DESERT STORM: THE WEAPONS OF WAR

ELIOT BRENNER AND WILLIAM HARWOOD AND THE EDITORS OF UPI

PHOTOGRAPHS BY REUTERS INTERNATIONAL NEWS SERVICE

ORION BOOKS / NEW YORK

✪ Design by Peter A. Davis and the Flyboys

Text Copyright © 1991 by United Press International
Photographs © 1991 by Reuters International News Service

Published by Orion Books, a division of Crown Publishers, Inc.
201 East 50th Street, New York, New York, 10022
Member of the Crown Publishing Group

ORION and colophon are trademarks of Crown Publishers, Inc.

Produced by Wieser & Wieser, Inc.
118 East 25th Street, New York, NY 10010
Manufactured in the United States of America

Library of Congress Catalog Number: 91-70475
ISBN: 0-517-58612-6

10 9 8 7 6 5 4 3 2 1

FIRST EDITION

CONTENTS

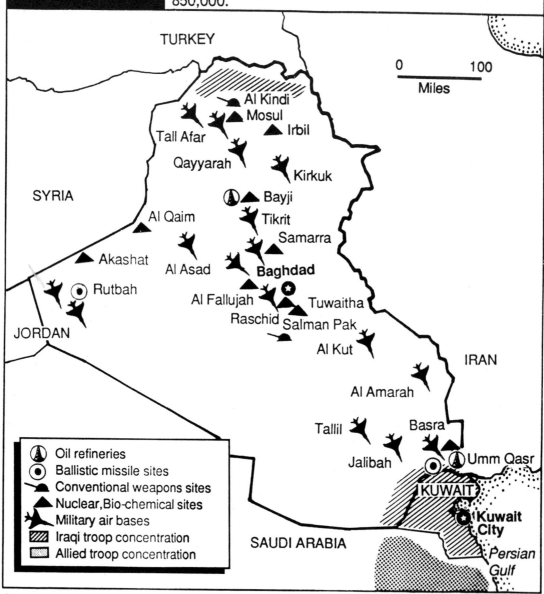

Key Iraqi Targets
Strategic Sites in Iraq

IRAQI FORCES

Seven corps. 55 to 60 divisions. 555,000 regular troops, 480,000 reserves believed to be mobilized.

Six divisions of Republican Guards. Iraq claims the Popular Army, its militia, is 8 million strong. Its true estimate is at around 850,000.

4,000 tanks, 2,700 armored personnel carriers, 3,000 artillery pieces and 500 combat aircraft support the forces.

There are reportedly more than 200 missiles of four types, Soviet made or modified versions

TURKEY

0   100
Miles

Al Kindi
Mosul
Irbil
Tall Afar
Qayyarah
Kirkuk
SYRIA
Bayji
Al Qaim
Tikrit
Samarra
Akashat
Al Asad
Baghdad
Rutbah
Al Fallujah
Tuwaitha
Raschid Salman Pak
JORDAN
Al Kut
IRAN
Al Amarah
Tallil
Basra
Jalibah
Umm Qasr
KUWAIT
Kuwait City
SAUDI ARABIA
Persian Gulf

Legend:
- Oil refineries
- Ballistic missile sites
- Conventional weapons sites
- Nuclear, Bio-chemical sites
- Military air bases
- Iraqi troop concentration
- Allied troop concentration

Source: Center for Defense Information

UPI Graphic

THE SEEDS OF WAR

Just a few hundred feet over southeastern Iraq, the cruise missile raced northwest toward its target after streaking like a white-hot comet through the night from a battleship in the Persian Gulf. From another point of the compass— unseen in the black of a moonless night and undetected by radars blinded by high technology—the Stealth fighter bored in. Operation Desert Shield had become Operation Desert Storm.

The Wild Weasels, Ravens and Prowlers raced to their targets, their electronic ears and eyes open, listening for the tell-tale sound of a SAM radar to be jammed or blown up by a HARM missile. Tomcats, Eagles, Hornets, Tornados and Jaguars closed on their targets, many in Baghdad itself. Farther back, for their protection, an AWACS Sentry watched over them all—the fighters, the bombers and the jammers—with the care of an orchestra conductor working through a symphony.

They followed what is said to be a 600-page daily script, only theirs was the first page in a battle pitting the best of the West's weaponry against

President George Bush is surrounded by a sea of U.S. servicemen as he greets the troops in Dhahran, Saudi Arabia. Bush came to spend Thanksgiving 1990 with American troops in the Gulf.

a massive accumulation of military might bought by Iraqi President Saddam Hussein for $50 billion.

Operation Desert Storm marked the beginning of the first microchip war, a battle of high-tech weaponry that is frighteningly accurate—witness television shots of gun camera film showing a bomb dropping into Iraqi air force headquarters in Baghdad—but not foolproof, as was demonstrated when some Scud ballistic missiles slipped past a hurriedly assembled Patriot air defense missile system and hit populated areas in Israel.

The start of the Persian Gulf war, then, marked a watershed in the history of combat, a transition between the age of the terrifying carpet bomb raid—although some of that was written into the score for good measure—to the impersonal wizardry of the computer age. But no matter how high-tech the weapons, control of contested real estate remained the ultimate goal, with both sides girding early on for a down and dirty fray that promised to be the tank engagement of all time, what Saddam at one point called "the mother of all battles."

What brought these awesome forces to bear in the hot, featureless sands of the Middle East? In a word, oil and the right of a small but

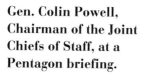

Gen. Colin Powell, Chairman of the Joint Chiefs of Staff, at a Pentagon briefing.

independent nation to be free. It was the physical manifestation of the world's anger over Saddam's brutal solution to an economic conflict with Kuwait as Iraq sought to rebuild from the Iran-Iraq war.

"The liberation of Kuwait has begun."
— Marlin Fitzwater, spokesman for U.S. President Bush

On Aug. 2, 1990, Saddam Hussein sent his tanks into tiny Kuwait, a Persian Gulf emirate that has dabbled with democracy over the years and is run by the Al Sabbah family. A stunned world watched as his Soviet-built tanks rumbled south into Kuwait City with its onion dome-like water towers.

The video tapes smuggled out showed a pearl of a Gulf city ground under the heel of a man President Bush later likened to a Middle Eastern Hitler. Refugees began streaming southward to the Saudi border town of Khafji, rushing through the customs house behind the chain link fence on the border and then down past the Khafji Beach Hotel that sits on the Gulf side of the north-south road that was later to be lined with artillery and anti-aircraft batteries.

Overhead, at least four Kuwaiti A-4 Skyhawk jets, aging planes bought from the United States, raced southward to safety. And to the west, in the nearer dunes and farther off hard-packed desert plain, Kuwaiti Army units dashed into Saudi Arabia.

The path down the coast heads straight to the major Saudi oil fields, refineries and both on-shore and off-shore loading facilities. The Saudi Arabian 65,000-plus military force likely would have been pounded into the sand had Iraq chosen to advance. And even if the Saudis could have moved firepower into the area quickly, which was unlikely, Iraq would already have been well on the way to controlling either directly or by intimidation a major portion of the world's oil reserves.

Defense Secretary Dick Cheney climbed into an executive jet for an appointment that would change the course of Middle East history. He sat down with Saudi King Fahd, laid out the latest spy satellite pictures of Iraqi tanks headed for Khafji and the lucrative oil fields just hours down the coastal road.

All right, said the king. *Send your troops to protect us.*

On Aug. 7, pilots of the U.S. Air Force 1st Tactical Fighter Wing got the order to head for Saudi Arabia. So rapidly were they and their tankers sent out over the Atlantic that there was no time for their support crews to precede them. The first aircraft to land belonged to the unit commander who taxied up to a parking place at a Saudi airbase, brought his twin-engine fighter-bomber to a halt, shut down the screaming turbines and reached behind his seat for nose wheel chocks.

President Saddam Hussein of Iraq salutes Islamic leaders at a gathering in Baghdad, four days before the United Nations deadline of January 15. The Iraqi leader told the assembly that all Moslems in the world should prepare to wage a holy war against Western forces gathered in the Gulf.

He jumped down to the concrete and raced to put the chocks in place before the airplane rolled off its mark when its hydraulic brakes shut down. Then he walked a few yards over, waved his wingman into place for a similar maneuver. The two of them then helped the third plane park. And so it went.

The planes marked the first trickle of a D-Day-like mobilization of American forces, a buildup that would reach at least 415,000 U.S. personnel and another 245,000 allied soldiers, sailors, Marines and airmen by the time hostilities broke out.

With the winds of war growing ever stronger, August gave way to September. Bush continued a marathon effort to enlist allies in the cause. Signing on were England, France, the tiny nations of the Gulf Cooperative Council, including Qatar and its 18-plane air force. Egypt and Syria, among others, committed Arab troops as well, making it clear that the effort was not just the infidel West against Saddam.

At the same time, vast naval armadas continued to gather off the shores of Saudi Arabia and Kuwait.

Once the U.S. and allied force was sufficiently large to deter any move by Iraq into Saudi Arabia, Bush made a decision that ultimately put the coalition on a collision course with Iraq for war. He ordered a doubling of U.S. forces, which by then had reached 230,000.

Then the United Nations took an eventful vote. On a tally of 12-2, with China taking a pass and agreeing not to veto the measure, the body authorized "all means necessary" to get Saddam out of Kuwait, setting a deadline of Jan. 15.

Saddam's elite Republican Guards dug themselves into positions along the Iraq-Kuwait border, positioning themselves in a region where U.S. forces might try an end run around Kuwait to surround the country. His forward troops in Kuwait built triangular defenses with the broad end facing south toward the massed allied troops. Before the sand walls were trenches filled with oil, tank traps, minefields and barbed wire.

His Soviet-built MiG-29s and French Mirage F-1 jets were at the ready, as were his top-of-the-line Soviet T-72 tanks.

The clock ticked down. Weaponry poured in. The diplomats got nowhere.

After a somber and solemn debate, both the House and Senate voted to authorize the use of force.

At 12:01 a.m. EST, Wednesday, Jan. 16, 1991, the United Nations deadline ran out. A 28-nation coalition and Saddam Hussein stood ready to do battle. It did not take long.

At 6:30 p.m. Washington time, 2:30 a.m. in sleepy Baghdad, the bombs began falling and the computerized maps stored in the brains of the Tomahawks led them precisely home.

The anti-aircraft guns sent up fire so thick it looked like the pilots could step from their cockpits and walk on it. The Stealth fighters slipped through the radars that the F-4G Wild Weasels were attacking and the EF-111 Ravens were jamming. And to the south, the E-3A Sentry Airborne Warning and Control planes were sorting out the air traffic, working through the sheet music of the first day of the war.

"The liberation of Kuwait has begun," said Fitzwater, reading a statement by Bush to reporters at the White House at 7 p.m.

Two hours later, speaking from the Oval Office, Bush declared, "The world could wait no longer."

"A lot of us are very glad it started because it is the beginning of an end."

- Airman 1st Class Stephanie Horsfall, 19, of Medina, Ohio, at a bomb assembly facility in Saudi Arabia.

Egyptian Special Forces soldiers stand at attention in front of M-60 tanks during arrival ceremonies in Saudi Arabia. Egypt sent the second largest contingent of troops among Arab states.

MANPOWER AND MATERIEL

2

The start of Operation Desert Storm opened a new chapter in the history of warfare, a conflict marking the first widespread use of advanced high-technology "smart" weapons to destroy military targets from the air with a minimum loss of civilian life. But with some 545,000 Iraqi troops dug into the heavily fortified sands of Kuwait behind razor wire, mine fields, booby traps and batteries of Soviet-made tanks and artillery, the United Nations coalition also had to be prepared to wage a more traditional "up-close-and-personal" ground war, a battle pitting veterans of a brutal eight-year war with Iran against untried allied forces equipped with superior weapons.

When President Bush ordered F-117A Stealth fighters, unmanned cruise missiles and other combat aircraft into Iraq to kick off Operation Desert Storm, the coalition had 680,000 troops and support personnel in the theater of combat. They consisted of 415,000 Americans and 245,000 from allied nations and members of the Gulf Cooperation Council with the majority coming from Saudi Arabia, Great Britain, France, Egypt

Opposite:
The 1st Cavalry Division, one of the Army's most potent fighting forces, arrived in the Gulf in October. Here soldiers unload a Bradley Fighting vehicle, an armored personnel carrier.

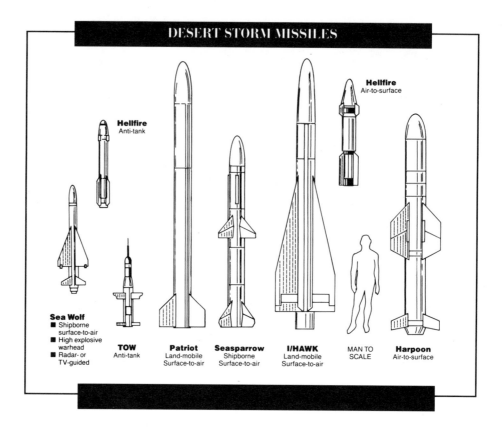

DESERT STORM MISSILES

Hellfire
Anti-tank

Hellfire
Air-to-surface

Sea Wolf
■ Shipborne
surface-to-air
■ High explosive
warhead
■ Radar- or
TV-guided

TOW
Anti-tank

Patriot
Land-mobile
Surface-to-air

Seasparrow
Shipborne
Surface-to-air

I/HAWK
Land-mobile
Surface-to-air

MAN TO
SCALE

Harpoon
Air-to-surface

and, surprisingly, Syria. The U.S. force was made up of 245,000 Army troops, 75,000 from the Marine Corps, 50,000 from the Navy and 45,000 representing the Air Force. Of that total, some 157,716 were reservists called up before the start of hostilities.

In terms of materiel, the allies fielded a formidable force indeed. The United States supplied some 500 cruise missiles, 1,700 helicopters and 1,800 fixed-wing aircraft, including top-of-the-line F-117A Stealth fighter-bombers, B-52 Stratofortresses, F-111 bombers, F-16 Fighting Falcons and F-15 Eagles, along with carrier-based Navy F-18 Hornets, A-6 Intruders and deadly F-14 Tomcats. On the ground, thousands of tanks and armored personnel carriers were deployed in the shifting sands of the Saudi Arabian desert, along with thousands of mobile artillery pieces, mines, anti-tank weapons, electronic countermeasure equipment and state-of-the-art satellite communications and reconnaissance gear.

The Patriot missile system was deployed in Saudi Arabia and, ultimately, Israel to protect ground forces from Iraqi Scud missiles. The Patriot system, untried in actual combat prior to the Gulf war, played a major role in the opening stages of the conflict, successfully using phased-array radar to track, intercept and destroy many incoming Scuds before they could strike their targets.

The centerpiece of America's ground force was the Abrams M-1A1 main battle tank, a 63-ton rolling fortress equipped with safeguards against chemical and biological warfare. Capable of firing a 120mm

As the war began, Iraq was estimated to have between 500 and 1,000 of these Soviet T-72 Tanks, their top-of-the-line ground warfare vehicles.

armor-piercing shell some 2.5 miles while rumbling across the desert at 20 mph, the M-1A1 is considered by many to be the most sophisticated battle tank in the world. The United States deployed 1,200 M-1A1 tanks on the front lines for Operation Desert Storm, with 700 chemically vulnerable M-1s held in reserve at the rear.

The Navy stationed 37 ships in the Persian Gulf, including two battleships—the USS Wisconsin and Missouri—and two aircraft carriers, the USS Midway and Ranger. While the awesome 16-inch guns of the battlewagons were not used in the initial attack on Iraq and Kuwait, Tomahawk cruise missiles were launched from the Wisconsin, the Missouri and at least one submarine during the opening stages of the war, knocking out high-priority targets with a precision that would have flabbergasted military planners just a few short years ago.

The Navy also stationed 32 vessels in the North Arabian Sea and the Gulf of Oman with another 26 ships patrolling in the Red Sea, including four aircraft carriers: the USS America, Roosevelt, Saratoga and Kennedy. Given the nuclear weapons presumably on board the carriers, it was the most powerful naval armada ever assembled for the conduct of war.

To keep tabs on the opposition, the United States used its fleet of spy satellites to survey the Persian Gulf theater of operations and to determine Iraqi troop movements, weapons placement and to help gather data for bomb damage assessments, or BDAs, to show military planners the results of bombing raids and which targets might need extra attention.

An F-117A stealth fighter flown by the 37th Tactical Fighter Wing out of Tonopah, Nevada. The F- 117 first saw action in the 1989 invasion of Panama. Its results there were mixed, but in the opening attacks of Desert Storm, the stealth plane proved highly effective.

A Saudi Arabian soldier kneels and prays to Mecca as Kuwaiti soldiers stand atop a Kuwaiti British-made Chieftain tank on the front lines. The Kuwaiti flag flies from the tank.

The orbits of two Defense Support Program—DSP—early warning satellites equipped with large heat-sensitive infrared telescopes reportedly were adjusted to maximize their ability to spot Scud launches, giving military and civilian authorities about 90 seconds warning of an impending attack. At least two and possibly three photo-reconnaissance satellites capable of seeing objects as small as 3 inches across were believed to be in service to help provide bomb damage assessments to military planners.

Cloudy weather disrupted such orbital surveillance during the first days of the war, but a radar imaging satellite known as Lacrosse presumably was able to continue spying on Iraq and Kuwait, possibly searching for mobile Scud missile launchers by using radar beams to "see" below the surface of the desert and into camouflaged trenches where they might have been hidden. Other signals intelligence satellites, or "sigints," likely were used to eavesdrop on Iraqi military communications from orbits 22,300 miles above the equator.

By default, the United States' major partner in Operation Desert Storm was Saudi Arabia, which provided critical logistical support and staging areas to coalition forces along with major elements of a 67,500-man army and air force. The Saudis, in total, fielded 550 battle tanks, including 50 American M-60A1s and 300 French AMX-30s, 1,100 M-113 armored personnel carriers and batteries of anti-tank weapons, mobile artillery pieces, Stinger and Redeye surface-to-air missiles. The 18,000-man Saudi air force was equipped with 189 combat aircraft, including three F-15 squadrons, Tornados and a full complement of American air-to-air and air-to-ground missiles. There were some 20,000 Saudi soldiers on the front lines when war broke out.

The aircraft carrier USS John F. Kennedy passes thorugh the Suez Canal on her way to the Red Sea. Five other U.S. warships were accompanying the John F. Kennedy. The Kennedy was one of four flat-tops sent to the Red Sea to suppelement U. S. air power in the region.

Great Britain fielded 27,000 combat troops and another 6,000 support personnel. According to the British Defense Ministry, 428 tanks were deployed in theater, 170 of them state-of-the-art Challengers attached to the famed "Desert Rats" of the 7th Armored Brigade. Other elements of the British artillery and ground force included 16 M-109 guns, 12 M-110 howitzers and batteries of surface-to-surface and surface-to-air missiles.

British airpower in the Persian Gulf included 3.5 squadrons of Tornado GR-1 warplanes, 1.5 squadrons of Tornado F-3s, one squadron of Jaguar fighter jets and 18 Gazelle helicopters. British authorities refused to say how many planes made up a squadron but the Center for Defense Information in Washington put the total number of British combat aircraft at 56 at the start of hostilities.

Egypt's President Hosni Mubarak sent about 35,000 troops to Saudi Arabia along with an estimated 400 tanks and 20 warplanes while Syria, once chastised in the West for supporting terrorism, deployed 20,000 troops in theater. France chipped in more than three dozen Mirage 2000s, Jaguar F-3s and Mirage F-1CR warplanes. Another two dozen French Puma helicopter gunships also were ordered to the Persian Gulf, along with 40 AMX-30 battle tanks and a naval task force consisting of 12 to 14 warships anchored by a guided missile cruiser and two guided missile destroyers. It was the largest overseas deployment of French troops since the Algerian War.

The remainder of the weapons and manpower—troops and civilians—arrayed against Saddam Hussein were supplied by more than two dozen nations and members of the Gulf Cooperation Council, made up of Saudi Arabia, Bahrain, Oman, the United Arab Emirates, Qatar and Kuwait.

Standing alone against the world and what appeared to be

A Saudi soldier walks atop a French-made Panhard AMX-30 tank.

overwhelming military firepower was the political will and military cunning of Saddam Hussein, Iraq's battle-hardened million-man army and an arsenal of high-powered but relatively low-tech weaponry.

"The Iraqis, Saddam Hussein, have a very large military force," Cheney said. "Depending upon what criteria you use, certainly one of the largest in the world; some have said the fourth largest in the world. In the last decade, he spent over $50 billion on armaments. The force possesses thousands of tanks, hundreds of aircraft, over a million men in uniform, missiles, etc."

Facing the United Nations coalition in Kuwait were 4,200 Iraqi tanks, 2,800 armored personnel carriers, 3,100 artillery pieces and an unknown number of French-built Mirage F-1 jet fighters and Soviet-built MiG-29s, -25s, -23s and -21s out of a total force of some 809 combat aircraft made up of 398 fighter-bombers and 411 interceptors. Adding in transport planes and helicopters, the total rises to about 1,400.

While the Iraqi navy posed a minimal threat to allied forces, Saddam Hussein also wielded Soviet FROG-7 battlefield missiles, Chinese-built Silkworm anti-ship missiles and French-made Exocet rockets. The deadly nature of the Exocet was demonstrated in 1987 when an Iraqi jet mistakenly fired on and heavily damaged the guided missile frigate USS Stark in the Persian Gulf, killing 37 sailors. And as the opening days of the war aptly demonstrated, Saddam's military machine was equipped with more Scud ballistic missiles than originally believed. While the rockets fired in the opening stages of the conflict on Saudi Arabia and Israel were ineffective against military targets, they had a powerful political effect, outraging the Israeli populace and creating a

United States M-1 tanks of 464 Delta Company. 1st Brigade, 24th Infantry, practice maneuvers in the Saudi Arabian desert. The allies hoped to avoid a bloody ground war, but feared that bombing alone would not dislodge Saddam's forces from Kuwait.

A soldier with the US Marines 1st Tank Battalion sits on the gun of his M-60 tank reading a book, January 16. A few hours after this picture was taken, Operation Desert Storm was unleashed.

strong pressure on Israel's government to enter the conflict - a move likely to splinter Bush's coalition.

In terms of manpower, an estimated 545,000 Iraqi regular army and reserve troops were dug in within the borders of Kuwait awaiting the expected coalition ground attack, relying on tank traps, rocket launchers, mine fields and other deadly surprises to offset the allies' advantage in technology. The elite Republican Guard, six divisions of highly nationalistic troops loyal to Saddam Hussein, was headquartered in Basra, just north of the Iraq-Kuwait border, and deployed throughout the region.

Iraq has "tanks, it has personnel carriers, it has air defense guns, it has very redundant, resilient communications between the different operating echelons of the army," said Gen. Colin Powell, chairman of the U.S. Joint Chiefs of Staff. "It has stockages of food, ammunition and parts with the army in theater. And they have a very elaborate supply system coming down from the interior of the country to sustain that army."

Iraq's army and air force, then, posed a stiff military challenge, making up one of the most powerful non-nuclear forces in the world. Taken as a whole, the Iraqi military machine consisted of:

- 955,000 combat troops including about 480,000 reserves.
- 5,500 main battle tanks, including 1,000 Soviet-built T-72s.
- 100 light tanks.
- 6,000 armored personnel carriers.
- About 3,000 artillery pieces.
- At least 36 and probably more mobile and fixed-base Scud-B

missile launchers (number of missiles unknown).
- 50 FROG-7 missile battlefield launchers.
- 160 surface-to-air (SAM) SA-2 missiles, 140 SA-3s, some 300 others.
- 4,000 air defense guns.
- A 5,000-man navy made up of five frigates, six corvettes, eight missile carriers, six torpedo boats, eight mine warfare units, six amphibious craft and two presidential yachts.
- 809 combat aircraft.
- An unknown number of paramilitary "people's army" irregulars.

And so, for the fifth time this century, the forces of a major war were unleashed and young men of many nations once again were thrust into harm's way after their elders' failure to resolve the conflict at the negotiating table.

An Iraqi Popular Army soldier during a weapon training in late September. Thousands of volunteers joined the Popular Army in the last weeks of 1990.

THE AIR WAR

3

The air war against Iraq was fought with the most diverse—and one of the most deadly—assortments of warplanes ever assembled. In fact, the runways at Saudi air bases took on the appearance of the Farnborough Air Show held each year in Great Britain: the racks of bombs and long-range fuel tanks held under shelters, the planes parked in every available parking space under corrugated roofs and in blast-hardened shelters.

The runways at Iraqi air bases took on the appearance of cratered moonscapes after relentless, around-the-clock bombardment by allied forces to cripple Saddam Hussein's air force, the most powerful in the region and a major threat to allied troops and civilians in Saudi Arabia and Israel.

The coalition air war was fought not only from bases strategically placed across Saudi Arabia but also from the sea and, interestingly enough, from below the sea in the form of submarine-launched cruise missiles, unmanned computer-controlled flying bombs capable of striking their

Opposite:
An F-14 Tomcat from Fighter Squadron 32 and an A-6E Intruder from Attack Squadron 75 attached to Carrier Air Wing 3, embarked on the USS John F. Kennedy, fly over the Saudi Arabian desert.

A Patriot tactical air defense missile launcher deployed on an air base in Saudi Arabia. The Patriots earned the nickname "Scudbusters" for their success in knocking down Saddam's ballistic missiles. The Patriot's 'umbrella of protection' covers roughly two square miles.

targets with pinpoint accuracy. In addition, a NATO base at Incirlik, Turkey, was used as a staging ground for fighter-escorted bombing runs by F-111s headed into northern and western Iraq.

The allied toolbox included a deadly mix of interceptors and strike aircraft, including F-117A Stealth fighters, agile F- 16s, heavily armed F-15s, radar-killing F-4s and carrier based A-6s, F-18s and F-14s along with Tomahawk cruise missiles and a smorgasbord of exotic weaponry ranging from laser-guided bombs to big, 2-ton ground pounders.

The American air power also included six aircraft carriers—the Midway and Ranger in the Persian Gulf and the Saratoga, Roosevelt, America and Kennedy in the Red Sea— contributing 450 aircraft to the coalition total.

But Saddam Hussein's arsenal included the Soviet-built Scud missile, a ballistic liquid-fueled rocket. Iraq's Scud launchers were among the highest priority targets in the allies' initial air strikes, but they proved harder to eliminate than first expected. Even after two weeks of allied air attacks, Saddam was able to launch Scuds at Israel and Saudi Arabia.

Scud Missile: The Scud is a Soviet-designed battlefield surface-to-surface ballistic missile that can be launched from fixed sites or mobile launchers. The Scud-B weighs 13,888 pounds, stands 37 feet tall and has a range of 180 miles. The Scud-C weighs 22,000 pounds, measures 40 feet long and has a range of 280 miles. Capable of carrying nuclear or conventional warheads, Iraqi Scuds were modified to increase their range. Allied officials feared the Iraqi versions were capable of carrying chemical or biological warheads as well. However, the Scuds' effectiveness was limited by their inaccuracy, and by the devastating success of the U. S. Patriot missiles.

Patriot Air Defense Missile: The 2,200-pound Patriot missile, which can be equipped with nuclear or conventional warheads, made an impressive battlefield debut in Operation Desert Storm, knocking Iraqi Scud missiles out of the sky before they could hit their targets. Equipped with a solid-fuel rocket motor, Patriot missiles are capable of speeds up to Mach 3 and range up to 43 miles. Four Patriots are mounted on a single mobile launcher. The key to their operation is a sophisticated phased-array radar, which detects and tracks incoming missiles and sends guidance data to an attacking Patriot. The rockets stand about 17 feet high and are 16 inches wide.

Despite the success of the Scud as a weapon of terror, Iraq seemed clearly out-gunned by American air power, bolstered by high-tech British Tornados, French Mirages and other allied aircraft. Such sophisticated delivery systems and state-of-the-art computer-controlled weaponry added up to an overwhelming combination of air power that quickly gave the allied coalition control of the sky over Kuwait and Iraq during the initial stages of the war.

ALLIED AIR POWER

U.S. AIR FORCE WARPLANES AND MISSILES

F-117A Stealth Fighter: The exotic-looking F-117A Stealth fighter is the first aircraft in the world designed from the ground up to elude radar detection. The 52,500-pound single-seat jet measures 65 feet 11 inches long, 12 feet five inches high and has a wingspan of 43 feet 4 inches. It is equipped with a redundant computer-assisted "fly-by-wire" flight control system and a sophisticated digital avionics package. F-117As are thought to be capable of using location and velocity data from Global Positioning System navigation satellites for inertial navigation.

Most operational details about the Stealth fighter are classified, but the aircraft is known to exhibit high subsonic performance. Bombs and other weapons are mounted on an internal carriage that apparently drops down into the airstream before deployment, but details about the F-117A's offensive and defensive systems are classified. The aircraft made its combat debut during the American invasion of Panama when two F-117As dropped 2,000-pound laser-guided bombs with mixed results. During Operation Desert Storm, F-117As reportedly struck targets in Baghdad with great precision.

To pave the way for the initial strike on Bagdhad and other high-priority targets in Iraq and Kuwait, Air Force F-4G advanced "Wild

An MPQ-53 missile guidance and control radar group for a Patriot air defense missile unit. One key to the Patriots' effectiveness was this sophis

F-4G Phantom "Wild Weasels" fly over the desert at sunset. In the dark of night on January 16, Wild Weasels were among the first U.S. planes into Iraq . Their job: to take out the enemy's air defense radar, an essential first step in establishing air superiority.

Weasel" jets were used to knock out enemy radar systems.

F-4G Phantom "Advanced Wild Weasel:" Designed in the 1950s and constantly upgraded, the F-4 is one of the meanest looking airplanes in the U.S. inventory with more than 1,000 still in service in Air National Guard units and around the world. But only the F-4G "Wild Weasel" is still in service with the active Air Force. Equipped with two 17,900-pound-thrust turbojet engines, the F-4 carries a crew of two—a pilot and a weapons officer—weighs 61,795 pounds fully loaded, has a wingspan of 38 feet 11 inches and measures 62 feet 11 inches long. F-4s are capable of flying twice the speed of sound at 40,000 feet with a range of more than 1,300 miles. The F-4G Wild Weasel is equipped with electronic warfare equipment designed to locate enemy radar-controlled anti-aircraft batteries and missile sites. It can be armed with AIM-7 and AIM-9 air-to-air missiles and HARM and Shrike anti-radar missiles. Standard F-4s can be equipped with Durandal anti-runway bombs, 1,000-pound "smart" bombs, cluster bombs and a variety of general purpose bombs weighing up to 2,000 pounds.

AIM-7 Sparrow and AIM-9 Sidewinder Missiles: Armament includes four radar-guided AIM-7 Sparrow missiles and four heat-seeking infrared sensitive AIM-9 Sidewinder missiles for air-to-air combat. These missiles measure about 10 feet long and fly faster than twice the speed of sound. Range varies from around 10 miles to 25 miles. The missiles can be easily

Two American F-15 jet fighters cross paths on the runway after exercises at a Saudi airbase. The F-15s are from the First Tactical Fighter Wing based at Langley Air Force Base, Virginia.

distinguished by the number of fins: the Sparrow has eight (four at the base and four at right angles around the midsection) while the Sidewinder has just four at the base.

HARM Missiles: To knock out enemy radar systems, F-4Gs are equipped with AGM-88 high-speed anti-radiation missiles known by the acronym HARM, which also can be carried by EF-111As, B-52 bombers and F-15 fighters. HARM missiles weigh 807 pounds, measure 13 feet 8.5 inches long and 10 inches in diameter. The missile is launched only after the F-4G crew detects and identifies a target using an APR-47 radar attack and warning system. Once on its way, the AGM-88 homes in on the enemy radar, destroying it with a high-explosive warhead.

Shrike Missiles: The Wild Weasel also is equipped with AGM-45 Shrike missiles, a 400-pound subsonic rocket built to knock out enemy radar installations with a 149-pound explosive warhead. Shrike missiles, which employ a passive radar detection system, measure 10 feet long, 8 inches wide with a wingspan of 3.25 feet.

Saudi Arabian Air Force ground personnel remove the engine from a U.S.-made F-15 fighter plane. A Saudi pilot flying an F-15 became the first allied airman to down two Iraqi planes in one day.

25

A major element of the coalition air force is the F-15 Eagle, an all-weather jet fighter capable of penetrating enemy defenses and handling any foreign fighter currently in production.

F-15 Eagle: The F-15E is a two-seat, 68,000-pound twin-engine jet designed for air-to-air combat and bombing missions deep in enemy territory. With engines powerful enough to accelerate the plane in a vertical climb, the F-15E is equipped with a high-resolution APG-70 radar system and carries pods featuring the "low altitude navigation and targeting infrared for night"—LANTIRN—target detection system as well as a "forward-looking infrared"—FLIR—system to locate and identify enemy targets during night missions. The F-15E has a wingspan of nearly 43 feet. It measures 63 feet 9 inches long and about 19 feet from the tarmac to the tip of its twin vertical stabilizers.

F-15s typically are armed with an internal M-61A1 20mm cannon, four AIM-7 Sparrows and four AIM-9 Sidewinder air-to-air missiles or eight AIM-120 AMRAAMs, advanced medium-range air-to-air missiles. It also can be equipped with AGM-65 TV-or infrared-guided Maverick missiles, AGM-88 HARM missiles and a variety of bombs, ranging from laser-guided Paveway II smart bombs to 2,000-pound Mark-84s and Rockeye cluster bombs.

AGM-65 Maverick Missile: Maverick missiles are carried by a wide variety of warplanes, including A-7 Corsairs, A-10 Thunderbolts, F-4 Phantoms, F-16 Falcons, F-15Es and F-111 bombers. Up to six Mavericks can be carried by a single aircraft in clusters of three under each wing. Two versions of the weapons system are in use: one uses a television system for guidance and the other uses a heat-sensitive imaging infrared system for use at night.

Before launching a Maverick, the pilot first selects a target on a cockpit television screen using an image from the missile. Once the target is locked in, the missile is launched and continues on without further direction from the pilot. Various combinations of imaging sensitivity, control software and warhead design currently are in use. The missiles weigh between 462 pounds and 670 pounds depending on warhead weight, measuring 8 feet 1 inch long and 1 foot in diameter. Top speed is supersonic and the missile has a range of up to 25 miles.

Gliding TV-Guided Smart Bomb: Modular gliding "smart" bombs come in several sizes and work in a similar fashion. The 2,450-pound GBU-15, for example, measures 12.8 feet long, 1.5 feet wide and has a wingspan of 4.9 feet. The unit is made up of a 2,000-pound Mark 84 bomb equipped with either a television or infrared targeting system that feeds an image back to the launching aircraft. The operator can either guide the bomb all the way to a target or order the weapon to home in on its own like some high-tech video game.

Laser-Guided Smart Bomb: Laser-guided bombs are equipped with sensor kits that allow the weapon to use laser beams fired from the attacking aircraft (or another friendly plane) to home in on their targets. Such smart bombs come in a variety of sizes and can be carried by virtually all U.S. strike aircraft.

Yet another major component of the U.S. Air Force commitment to Operation Desert Storm is the F-16 fighter, developed as a replacement for the venerable F-4.

F-16 Fighting Falcon: The F-16 is one of the most maneuverable jet fighters ever built, capable of withstanding nine times the force of gravity in steep turns with internal fuel tanks loaded. In fact, the F-16 is more than capable of subjecting its pilot to such extreme forces that loss of consciousness can occur. The most current versions can be equipped with HARM and Shrike anti-radiation missiles as well as AMRAAMs, the LANTIRN night attack pod, a Global Positioning System satellite navigation system, advanced radar and electronic countermeasures equipment, up to six AIM-9 infrared air-to-air missiles, Mavericks and a variety of general purpose and smart bombs.

The F-16 is a Mach 2 fighter with a combat ceiling higher than 50,000 feet and a combat range of 340 miles. Equipped with an M-61A1 20mm cannon and 500 rounds of ammunition, the Fighting Falcon has a 32-foot 8-inch wingspan and measures 49 feet 5 inches long. It weighs up to 42,300 pounds and is powered by a single turbofan engine generating up to 27,600 pounds of thrust.

Along with a suite of fighters and attack jets, the Air Force also supplied heavy bombers to the Operation Desert Storm campaign, the B-52 Stratofortress and the F-111 tactical strike aircraft.

F-111 Tactical Strike Aircraft: The F-111 comes in three major varieties: a tactical strike aircraft (F-111F), an electronic jamming platform (EF-111A Raven) or a medium-range strategic bomber (FB-111A). These sleek jets are equipped with variable-sweep wings allowing them to reach speeds of Mach 1 at sea level and twice the speed of sound at 40,000 feet. With the wings set at full forward, the F-111 is capable of flying low and slow, making short take offs and landings. With wings swept back a maximum 72.5 degrees, the plane is capable of supersonic

F-16C Fighting Falcon aircraft from the 421st Tactical Fighter Squadron, from Hill Air Force Base, Utah. One of the most agile jets ever built, the F-16 can generate such G-forces in a turn that pilots must wear special pressurized suits to prevent them from blacking out.

flight. Another unique feature of the F-111 is the cockpit. The two-man crew sits side-by-side in an air-conditioned, pressurized module that also serves as an ejection pod equipped with parachutes and airbags to cushion impact. The floating ejection module even works under water. Pilots say the F-111 cockpit is one of the most uncomfortable in the U.S. inventory.

The 100,000-pound F-111 is powered by two turbofan engines with thrust levels ranging from 18,000 pounds (F-111A) up to 25,100 pounds (F-111F). The planes measure 75 feet 7 inches long, stand 17 feet 1 inch high and have wingspans of 32 feet (wings swept back) or 63 feet (wings swept forward). With a range of more than 3,100 miles, the F-111 can operate at Mach 1.2 at sea level, up to Mach 2.5 at its operational ceiling of 60,000 feet.

Armament for the FB-111 can include six nuclear bombs (two internally and four mounted on wing pylons) or supersonic AGM-69A short-range attack missiles, or SRAMs, that are internally guided and immune to jamming (not used in Operation Desert Storm). Other versions of the aircraft can carry up to 31,500 pounds of conventional weaponry. The EF-111 Raven, used during the initial strikes on Bagdhad, is equipped with an ALQ-99E jamming system, allowing its crew to suppress an enemy's electronic defenses. The Raven also features electronic defenses borrowed from the FB-111, the ALQ-137 and ALR-62 electronic countermeasures gear. The F-111 tactical strike aircraft can

Two United States Marines F-18 Hornet fighter planes refuel in flight with a Marine KC-130 tanker over the Gulf. The planes are refueled every 60 to 90 minutes to stay on constant alert. The tanker gives them 300 gallons per minute.

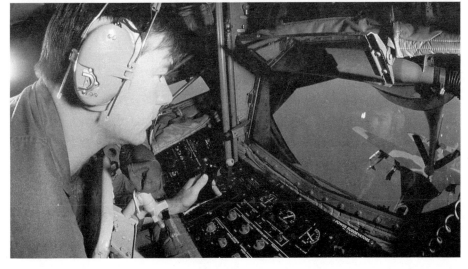

A boom operator's view from a KC-135 tanker during aerial refueling of an F-111.

carry conventional or nuclear bombs, or up to 12 French Durandal anti-runway bombs.

Durandal Anti-Runway Bomb: Durandal anti-runway bombs typically are launched about 185 feet up at speeds up to 685 mph. The bomb is slowed by a parachute that aims the nose straight down at the target. At that point, a rocket fires, driving the warhead nearly 16 inches into concrete targets before it detonates.

To knock out "hardened" targets and to demoralize ground troops, few weapons of modern conventional warfare have the ground-pounding impact of the huge B-52 bomber, capable of raining terror and destruction from 7 miles up.

B-52 Stratofortress: In Operation Desert Storm, B-52s were used for deadly carpet-bombing raids on the headquarters of Saddam Hussein's elite Republican Guard in and around Basra near the Iraq-Kuwait border.

The giant eight-engine, 488,000-pound B-52 first flew in 1954. That it is still flying in active service is a testament to its designers and an aggressive program to constantly upgrade the big warbirds to adapt them

Two A-7E's from Light Attack Squadron 72, embarked on board the USS John F. Kennedy. This is the last operational deployment of the A-7, which is currently being replaced by the F/A-18.

An F-117A Stealth fighter being refueled by a KC-135 Stratotanker.

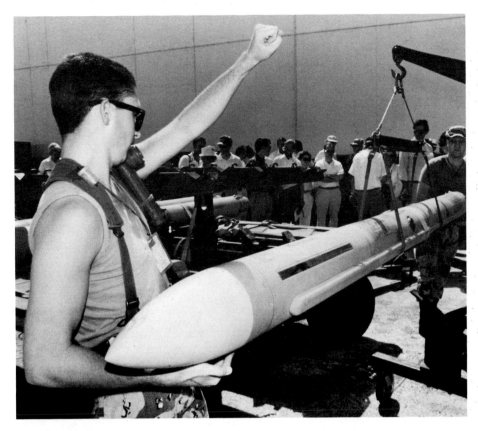

United States Air Force personnel move a Sidewinder AIM-7 missile into position for cleaning. The missiles are then placed back on F-15 fighters. In this picture, taken during the 1990 buildup, an American Congressional delegation watches in the background.

to a variety of combat missions, including a key role in Operation Desert Storm. Capable of carrying some 70,000 pounds of ordnance, including AGM-86 cruise missiles, gravity bombs and AGM-69A SRAMs, the B-52 is powered by eight 17,000-pound- thrust engines (B-52H). It has a wingspan of 185 feet, measures about 160 feet long and stands 40 feet 8 inches tall. Top speed is about 650 mph with an operational ceiling of 50,000 feet. With a crew of six, the B-52G model has a range of 7,500 miles while the B-52H can fly up to 8,800 miles without refueling.

All active B-52s are equipped with advanced avionics, including forward-looking infrared (FLIR) low-light viewing systems, ground-hugging terrain contour matching (TERCOM) guidance, satellite communications and a full suite of electronic countermeasures and attack warning gear. Armament varies according to mission, but B-52G/H models can carry eight SRAMs on wing pylons and conventional nuclear bombs inside the plane's bomb bay, or 12 AGM-86B air launched cruise missiles if SRAMS are excluded. The B-52G model can carry a full load of conventional weapons, including a dozen Harpoons. Its conventional bombs include the 500-pound Mark 82, the 750-pound Mark 83 and the 2,000-pound Mark 84.

AGM-84A Harpoon Anti-Ship Missile: The AGM-84A is a jointly developed Navy-Air Force missile designed to knock out enemy ships

A view from the cockpit of an A-7E Corsair, from Light Attack Squadron 72 on the carrier USS John F. Kennedy, training for low-level flight

using a radar homing system and a 488-pound high explosive. Up to 12 Harpoons can be carried by a single B-52G. With a range of more than 57 miles, Harpoons are powered by a 660-pound-thrust jet engine and measure 12 feet 7.5 inches long, 1 foot 1.5 inches wide and weigh 1,145 pounds.

A-7 Corsair II: The A-7 originally was built to serve as a Navy carrier-based attack aircraft, a role it still fulfills today. The Air Force version has been in service since 1968 as an air- to-surface attack plane capable of carrying a deadly variety of weapons weighing up to 15,000 pounds. The A-7 also is equipped with automatic flight controls, electronic countermeasures gear and an M-61A1 Vulcan 20mm machine gun that can be fired at up to 6,000 rounds per minute. The A-7, with its gaping jet air intake just under the cockpit, is powered by a single turbofan engine developing 13,390 pounds of thrust. The plane weighs up to 42,000 pounds when loaded and measures 45 feet 7 inches long and 16.75 feet tall with a wingspan of 38 feet 9 inches. Its combat range is 715 miles fully loaded.

Along with its fighters, bombers and ground attack aircraft, the Air Force also supplied a variety of other aircraft to Operation Desert Storm for reconnaissance, observation, refueling and transport, including planes loaded with electronic gear to monitor coalition and enemy air traffic.

E-3 Sentry Airborne Warning and Control System (AWACs): The E-3 Sentry is a modified Boeing 707 with a 30-foot-wide, 6-foot-thick disk-shaped rotating radar antenna mounted atop twin pylons 11 feet over the rear fuselage. Able to detect low-flying aircraft more than 200 miles away, even farther for higher-flying planes, the E-3 AWACs can locate, identify and track hundreds of targets at once and direct friendly warplanes to intercept incoming aircraft. The E-3, which can stay

A UH-60 Blackhawk helicopter from the 101st Airborne Division (air assault) on a mission over the Saudi Arabian desert.

airborne for more than 11 hours without refueling, typically operates at above 29,000 feet at speeds of more than 500 mph with a four-man flight crew and 13 to 19 radar and communications specialists. The 325,000-pound 707 is equipped with four turbofan engines generating 21,000 pounds of thrust each. Ten AWACs were in use for Operation Desert Storm, five representing the U.S. Air Force and five owned by Saudi Arabia.

U.S. NAVY AND MARINE WARPLANES AND MISSILES

Carrier-based warplanes were a major element of Operation Desert Storm, bolstering allied inventories by some 450 aircraft. In addition, Tomahawk cruise missiles launched from the USS Wisconsin, the USS Missouri and a submerged submarine gave the coalition a high-precision weapon that could be sent into highly defended areas without risking the life of a pilot.

A sailor pushes two 500-pound bombs past fighter planes on the deck of the USS Independence in the Gulf of Oman. These are free-fall bombs with a 'high-drag' crackle finish. In the background, with wings folded up, is an A-6 Intruder, one of the best all-weather attack aircraft in the coalition arsenal.

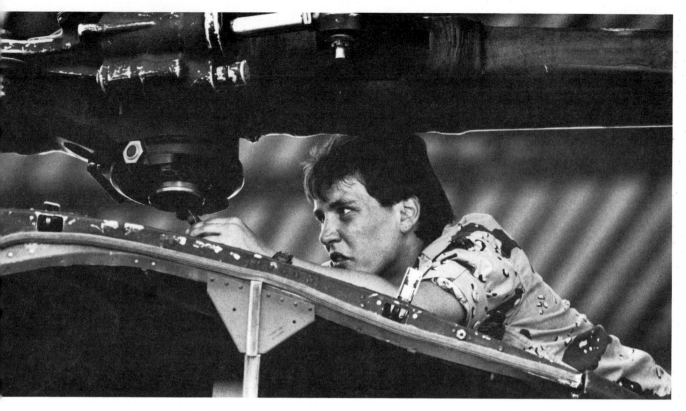

Tina Shields of Jacksonville, Florida, lies atop a newly arrived CH-47 helicopter as she assembles the rotor blades at a Saudi airport.

Tomahawk Cruise Missiles: Operation Desert Storm began with the launchings of Tomahawk cruise missiles from the battleships Missouri and Wisconsin. Later, at least one Tomahawk was launched from a submerged submarine within the first week of aerial combat. These super-accurate weapons are 18 feet 3 inches in flight (20 feet 6 inches with booster rocket) and 20.4 inches in diameter with a wingspan of 8 feet 9 inches. Initial propulsion is provided by a solid-fuel booster rocket after which a small turbojet engine takes over.

The Tomahawks used against Iraq feature a TERCOM guidance system that compares local topography with images stored in its computer memory as the ground-hugging missiles streak toward their targets up to 690 miles away. The missiles are amazingly accurate, difficult to detect and are capable of flying at extremely low altitudes, making them ideal for use against heavily defended targets that pose too great a risk for manned aircraft. It was a Tomahawk that, with astonishing precision, struck the headquarters of the Iraqi air force in downtown Baghdad.

F/A-18 Hornet (Navy and Marine Corps): The Hornet is a single-seat high-performance carrier-based jet strike fighter powered by two turbofan engines generating 16,000 pounds of thrust each. Top speed with a full load of armaments is subsonic, Mach 1.8 at altitude and without weapons. The F/A-18 is easily identified by its twin vertical tail fins, which are slightly canted outward toward the wings. The aircraft has a wingspan of

37 feet 5 inches, a length of 56 feet and it stands 15 feet 3 inches tall (ground to vertical fin tip). Maximum carrier takeoff weight 51,900 pounds.

The Hornet was built to serve as either a fighter or an attack jet, the first American warplane capable of performing both roles. For fighter missions, the F/A-18 can be equipped with a full load of AIM-7 Sparrow and AIM-9L and AIM-9J Sidewinder air-to-air missiles. For ground attack missions, the aircraft can be loaded with a variety of weapons, including 10 Mark 82 Snakeye bombs, nine Mark-83s or four 2,000-pound Mark 84s. It also can carry Durandal anti-runway bombs, HARM and Maverick missiles, cluster bombs and LAU- 61A/A rocket pods as well as an assortment of guided bombs.

Because of its dual role, the F/A-18 has one of the most complex cockpits in the world. The plane is equipped with a forward-looking infrared—FLIR—pod for night combat.

F-14 Tomcat: The Tomcat, star of the movie Top Gun, is a versatile carrier-based fighter equipped with two afterburning turbofan engines generating 20,900 pounds of thrust each. Equipped with variable-sweep wings, the twin-seat F-14 can track up to 24 targets at once with an advanced water-cooled AWG-9 fire control radar system and attack the six most threatening aircraft with long range AIM-54A Phoenix missiles at up to 100 miles away. It also is equipped with four AIM-9J Sidewinders, four AIM-7 Sparrow air-to-air missiles and one M-61A1 Vulcan cannon. The F-14 measures 62 feet 9 inches long and stands 16 feet high. Its wingspan varies between 64.1 feet to 38 feet when the wings are fully swept back. Maximum takeoff weight is 69,800 pounds, but Tomcats typically weigh in at about 55,000 pounds for fighter missions.

AGM-54A Phoenix Missile: The Phoenix is the most advanced air-to-air missile in the world, working in tandem with the F-14s sophisticated AWG-9 fire control system to seek out and destroy enemy warplanes at distances of up to 100 miles. Measuring 13 feet long and 15 inches wide, the Phoenix weighs 985 pounds and carries a 132-pound warhead. It is equipped with a slow-burning solid-fuel motor giving it a range of more than 120 miles at speeds up to Mach 5.

A-6 Intruder/Prowler: Three versions of the plane are in service in Operation Desert Storm: the KA-6D fuel tanker, the A-6E Intruder all-weather attack plane and the EA-6B Prowler, an electronic warfare platform carrying sophisticated jamming equipment and HARM anti-radiation missiles. All three are carrier based and have the same general teardrop-shape appearance, but the Prowler carries a crew of four in an expanded cockpit and sports an instrument-studded tail fin. The Intruder carries two crew members who sit side by side.

The Intruder is a subsonic aircraft featuring digital computer control, solid-state weapons release systems, FLIR infrared gear and a laser designator. Maximum carrier takeoff weight is 58,600 pounds with a ceiling of 40,600 feet and a maximum speed of about 647 mph using two 9,300-pound-thrust jet engines. The Intruder can be equipped with a variety of weapons, including AGM-65A Maverick missiles, AGM-84A Harpoon anti-ship missiles, Rockeye cluster bombs, AGM-109 cruise missiles and general purpose bombs weighing up to 500 pounds. The A-6E measures 54 feet 8 inches long, 15 feet 6 inches tall and has a wingspan of 53 feet.

The Prowler is equipped with three electronic warfare systems: on-board receiving sensors, a tactical jamming system with sensors mounted in a pod at the tip of the plane's tail fin and AGM-88A HARM anti-radiation missiles. The crew is made up of a pilot and three officers to operate the electronic warfare equipment. The Prowler measures 59 feet 10 inches long, 16 feet 3 inches high and has a wingspan of 53 feet. Maximum carrier takeoff weight is 58,600 pounds.

A-4 Skyhawk (Navy and Marine Corps): The A-4 is a single-seat attack bomber that first flew in 1954 and remained in production for 26 years. It can be equipped with AIM-9 air-to-air missiles, AGM-62A Walleye TV- guided glide bombs, AGM-65A Mavericks and a variety of bombs weighing up to 2,000 pounds. Skyhawks typically are equipped with two 20mm cannon and are powered by a single turbojet engine with thrust levels up to 11,200 pounds. The A-4 is 40 feet long, 15 feet tall and has a wingspan of 27 feet 6 inches. The plane weighs a maximum of about 27,000 pounds.

AGM-62 Walleye Bomb: Walleye guided bombs were described by the Navy in 1969 as "the most accurate and effective air-to-surface conventional weapon ever developed anywhere." The weapon is particularly simple to operate. Using a television camera in the nose of the bomb, the pilot first identifies the target on a cockpit TV screen and aims the bomb camera at the objective. Once the bomb is "locked" onto the target, it is released. Guidance is automatic, but the pilot can take manual control if necessary. Once release, the bomb also can be guided by a second aircraft crew, freeing the plane that dropped the bomb to make a quick getaway.

AV-8B Harrier II: The Harrier is unique among allied attack jets in that it can take off and land vertically like a helicopter or use very short runways. Based on a British design, the Harrier is equipped with a

Opposite:
A. U.S. Marine Corps Harrier jet takes off from the flight deck of the USS Nassau. With their vertical takeoff and landing (VTOL) ability, Harriers were likely to be used for close air support of ground forces.

22,000-pound-thrust engine and has a wingspan of 30 feet 4 inches. It is 46 feet 4 inches long and stands 11 feet 9 inches tall. Maximum vertical takeoff weight is about 19,500 pounds; maximum short takeoff weight: about 29,750 pounds. Standard equipment includes dual television/laser target acquisition gear and provisions for a wide variety of bombs and missiles, including rocket pods, smart bombs, Harpoons, Mavericks, cluster bombs and general purpose bombs weighing up to 2,000 pounds.

E-2C Hawkeye: The carrier-based, turboprop E-2C Hawkeye is the

Navy equivalent of the Air Force E-3 Sentry AWACs airborne control center, able to locate and track enemy aircraft and to direct F-14 Tomcats to intercept threatening warplanes. Working in concert with AEGIS cruisers, the E-2C plays a critical role in protecting American carrier battle groups. The E-2C Hawkeye is 18 feet 3 inches long, has a wingspan of 80 feet 17 inches and weighs up to 53,000 pounds. It carries a crew of five.

OTHER ALLIED WARPLANES AND MISSILES

European-built Tornados, French Mirages and joint French-British Jaguars joined U.S.-built aircraft deployed in Operation Desert Storm. Mirages and Jaguars also were in use by the Iraqi air force.

Panavia Tornado: A joint British, German, Italian project, the Tornado comes in several models, including a two-seat strike aircraft and a long-range interceptor. Tornado bombers from Britain's Royal Air Force had a crucial role in the opening phase of Desert Storm, streaking over Iraqi airbases at night. Navigating automatically by computer tape, the Tornados flew hugging the ground, in complete radio silence to avoid detection. They dropped bombs to crater the runways and simultaneously scattered mines to hinder the Iraqis from repairing the damage. The Tornado strikes were very effective, but at a high cost, because the airfields were heavily defended against low-flying planes. Some fifteen percent of Britain's Tornados in the Gulf were downed in the first two weeks of the war.

The swept-wing aircraft are powered by twin 16,000-pound-thrust turbofan engines and weigh in at more than 47,500 pounds (maximum weight is classified). Tornados have a top speed of more than Mach 2 unloaded and a range of about 375 miles with a typical load of weapons. The strike version can carry more than 90 types of ordnance weighing up to 18,000 pounds and is equipped for all-weather combat behind enemy lines.

Armament includes a pair of 27mm IWKA-Mauser machine guns and a remarkable variety of air-to-air and air-to-ground missiles along with laser-guided smart bombs, JP-233 anti- runway bombs, general purpose bombs of various weights and others. The aircraft measures 54 feet 9.5 inches long and 18 feet 8.5 inches tall from the runway to the top of the single tail fin. The wingspan varies between 45 feet 7.25 inches when fully open to 28 feet 2.5 inches when swept back.

JP-233 Anti-Runway Bomb: The JP-233 is a bomb container capable of

Opposite: **Meet the Warthog. Capt. Jim Glasgow enters his A-10 Thunderbolt anti-tank airplane. Under its nose is the barrel of an Avenger cannon. which fires slugs nearly the size of a soft-drink bottle at a velocity of 3,500 feet per second.The 23rd Tactical Fighter Wing, to which the plane belongs, is related to the Flying Tigers of WW II, hence the painting on the nose.**

dispensing by parachute small bomblets such as anti-runway explosives or anti-personnel mines. The JP-233 also accommodates anti-personnel mines designed to hinder runway repairs. The weapon system can be used by U.S. F-16s, F-111s and European Jaguars and Harriers, but the Tornado is the only aircraft that can carry both anti-runway and anti-personnel loads at one time using a large pod under the belly of the aircraft.

The Tornado interceptor is a British development and is considered one of the most efficient such aircraft in the world. The engines, airframe and other critical systems are identical with the strike version but its avionics and weapons systems are completely different. The Tornado interceptor can carry ASRAAM, AIM-9L Sidewinders and AIM-120 AMRAAM air-to-air missiles along with 1,000-pound bombs. The interceptor saw extensive action in the opening days of Operation Desert Storm.

Mirage F-1: The French Mirage F-1 is a single-seat multi-role jet capable of air-to-air combat, all-weather bombing missions and reconnaissance using an after-burning engine generating a maximum thrust of 15,873 pounds. The needle-nose F-1 has a wingspan of 27 feet 6.75 inches and weighs up to 33,510 pounds, measuring about 49 feet long and standing about 14 feet 10 inches tall. The Mirage F-1 has a maximum speed of better than twice the speed of sound at high altitude without a full load of weapons and an operational range of about 560 miles when loaded. Equipped with a sophisticated radar system, the F-1 can carry up to 8,820 pounds of weaponry, including two 30mm DEFA-5-53 cannon, Matra 550 Magic and AIM-9L Sidewinder air-to-air missiles, Durandal anti-runway bombs and various other conventional bombs.

Magic Missiles: The Magic is a close-range air-to-air missile measuring 9 feet long and 6.2 inches wide. At launch, the Magic weighs just 198 pounds. The missile has a top speed of about Mach 3 and a range of up to 6.2 miles. The 27.6-pound warhead explodes on contact with the target.

Mirage 2000: The Mirage 2000 is a sophisticated air-superiority fighter powered by a single turbojet engine developing 19,840 pounds of thrust with afterburner. Maximum speed with a full load of weapons is roughly 700 mph, although it can do better than Mach 2 when unloaded. The Mirage 2000 can be distinguished by its broad 29-foot 6-inch delta wing and dual air intakes on either side of the cockpit. The aircraft measures 47 feet long and weighs a maximum of 36,375 pounds; actual combat weight typically runs about 21,000 pounds. A variety of weapons can be accommodated, including Exocet anti-ship missiles, ASMP cruise missiles, Durandal bombs, air-to-air missiles and conventional bombs.

Exocet Anti-Ship Missile: The French-built Exocet is a surface-to-surface or air- launched all-weather anti-ship missile with a cylindrical body and a pointed nose. Originally designed as a ship- launched missile, the Exocet later was adapted for launch from aircraft. Flying at a sea-skimming altitude of just 8 feet or so, the missile's inertial guidance system carries it within range of a target ship after which active radar guidance takes over. An Exocet fired from an Argentine plane in the 1982 Falklands war hit the HMS Sheffield, starting a fire that ultimately sank the ship. An Exocet mistakenly fired by an Iraqi jet in 1987 heavily damaged the guided missile frigate USS Stark in the Persian Gulf, killing 37 men. The missile measures 15 feet 4.5 inches long and 13.75 inches wide. At launch, the Exocet weighs 1,444 pounds and has a range of up to 44 miles. The warhead weighs 364 pounds.

Jaguar: Like the Tornado, the Jaguar is an international combat aircraft, developed jointly by Great Britain and France. The Jaguar weighs up to 34,612 pounds and is powered by two Rolls Royce turbofan engines generating up to 8,400 pounds of thrust each. A wide variety of weaponry can be accommodated, up to 10,500 pounds, including AIM-9B Sidewinders and Matra 550 Magic air-to-air missiles, Durandal and JP-233 anti- runway bombs, Exocet anti-ship missiles, laser-guided smart bombs and various rockets. The Jaguar is about 51 feet long and 16 feet high with a wingspan of 28 feet 6 inches. With a top speed of a bit more than Mach 1.5 when unloaded, the Jaguar has an operational range of about 530 miles when loaded with weapons.

IRAQI AIR POWER

At the start of Operation Desert Storm, the 40,000-man Iraqi air force fielded 809 combat aircraft, including six squadrons of bombers, 22 squadrons of ground attack aircraft and 17 squadrons of fighter jets, including 30 Soviet MiG (Mikoyan-Gurevich)-29s, 25 MiG-25 Foxbats, 150 MiG-21s and 30 Mirage F-1s (described earlier). Iraq fielded one squadron of 12 reconnaissance jets (5 MiG 21s and seven MiG-25s) and two squadrons of Soviet-built transport planes.

MiG-29 Fulcrum: This multi-role attack-fighter is a top-of-the-line Soviet- built twin-engine jet capable of flying faster than twice the speed of sound when unloaded, an agile, fast-turning combat aircraft with a wide range of capabilities. Powered by two afterburning engines

The heat is on. Standing by a Patriot missile launcher, Sgt. James Parnell of El Paso, Texas (right), wipes his face while talking with Sgt. Clifton Bynum of Rocky Mountain, North Carolina.

generating a thrust of more than 17,000 pounds, the MiG-29 measures about 51 feet long, has a wingspan of some 39 feet and is believed to weigh about 36,800 pounds when fully loaded with fuel and weapons. Armament includes six air-to-air missiles.

MiG-25 Foxbat: The MiG-25 can be used as either a high-altitude interceptor or a reconnaissance platform with an operational ceiling of more than 88,000 feet using two afterburning turbojet engines generating up to 24,250 pounds of thrust each. The MiG-25 was developed by the Soviet Union to counter the ill-fated U.S. B-70 strategic bomber, which was canceled in 1961. As such, it is capable of flying very high and very fast. The MiG-25 is 78 feet long, has a wingspan of about 45 feet and weighs up to 79,800 pounds. It can carry a wide variety of Soviet air-to-air missiles, including the short-range AA-6 Acrid and the medium-range AA-7 Apex.

AA-6 Acrid: A medium to long-range air-to-air missile, the Acrid was designed in the late 1950s to counter the B-70. As such, it is the largest such missile in the world, measuring 21 feet long, 15.7 inches wide and weighing about 1,765 pounds. The AA-6 uses both radar homing and heat-seeking infrared technology to destroy targets within about 50 miles for the former and 15.5 miles for the latter.

AA-7 Apex: Equipped with four large delta wings, the Apex is another medium- to long-range air-to-air missile. It measures 15 feet long, about 8 inches wide and weighs some 700 pounds at launch. The Apex is believed to come in infrared and radar homing versions with a range of up to 25 miles.

MiG-23: The MiG-23 is a multi-role fighter with variable-sweep wings, two 22,485-pound-thrust afterburning turbofan engines and a top speed (unloaded) of Mach 2.3 at 36,000 feet. Its operational range when loaded with ordnance is about 560 miles with a service ceiling of 61,000 feet. The MiG-23 is equipped with electronic gear allowing it to detect aircraft up to 53 miles away, it is believed, and to lock onto targets at a range of about 34 miles. Soviet export models, however, are thought to have a less-powerful avionics package. The aircraft carries one GSh-23 machine gun with 500 rounds of ammunition and can carry AA-8 Aphid and AA-2 Atoll heat-seeking air-to-air missiles.

AA-8 Aphid: First seen in 1976, the Aphid, a short-range air-to-air missile, was first seen in 1976. It measures just 7 feet long and 4.7 inches wide, tipping the scales at just 121 pounds at launch. The missile has a range of about 3 miles and a 13-pound warhead.

AA-2 Atoll: Another close-range air-to-air missile, the Atoll closely resembles the U.S. AIM-9 Sidewinder, with radar homing and infrared capability. The Atoll measures 9 feet long, 4.7 inches wide and weighs about 154 pounds at launch. It has a range of about 4 miles and carries a 13-pound warhead.

MiG-21: Fast and agile, the MiG-21 single-seat single-engine fighter carries a relatively small number and load of weapons and is not equipped with modern instrumentation. But it is considered highly reliable and can make up to six sorties a day for several days in a row. The MiG-21 weighs up to 20,725 pounds when fully loaded with fuel and armament, measures 51 feet 8.5 inches long and has a wingspan of 23 feet 5.5 inches. The aircraft has been equipped with a variety of engines and has a top speed of just over Mach 2 with an operational service ceiling of about 50,000 feet. Typical armament includes: AA-2-2 Atoll and AA-8 Aphid advanced air- to-air missiles, rocket launchers, up to 48 types of bombs, including nuclear, chemical, napalm and fuel-air explosives, and a GSh-23 machine gun loaded with 200 rounds of ammunition.

Sukhoi Su-7: The Soviet-built Su-7 first flew in 1955. It is a large, powerful ground-attack warplane equipped with a 21,164-pound- thrust afterburning engine for a top speed of just over Mach 1 and an operational service ceiling of about 50,000 feet. But the Su-7 carries a relatively small weapons load, its fuel consumption is high and its combat radius (when loaded with weapons) is just 200 to 300 miles. On the other hand, the Su-7 is extremely tough and reliable and very easy to fly, making it a popular aircraft among pilots. Weapons include two NR-30 machine guns, rocket launchers, various conventional bombs, BETAB-250 anti-runway bombs and AA-2 Atoll heat-seeking air-to-air missiles. Many Su-7s still in service are equipped with an avionics system first installed in 1959.

Su-20 Fitter: The Su-20 is the export version of the Soviet Union's Su-17 ground attack fighter. The Soviet version is equipped with variable-sweep wings and a single afterburning turbojet engine generating a maximum 27,500 pounds of thrust. The Su-20 measures about 52 feet long and weighs a maximum of 42,330 pounds when fully loaded with fuel and weapons. Armament includes two NR-30 machine guns, Atoll and Aphid air-to-air missiles and various other weapons.

A MiG-29 Fulcrum viewed from front and back. At the beginning of the war, the Iraqi air force had 30 of these top-of-the-line Soviet multi-role attack-fighters.

An F-14 Tomcat races over the desert, its wings fully swept back for maximum speed.

Su-24 Fencer: An advanced, all-weather attack plane, the Su-24 is roughly based on the design of the American F-111 bomber with two side-by-side cockpit seats and variable-sweep wings. First flight was in 1970. The Su-24, also built in the Soviet Union, weighs up to 87,080 pounds when fully loaded with weapons and fuel and measures about 69 feet 10 inches long and 18 feet high with an estimated wingspan ranging from 56 feet 6 inches (wings swept forward) to 33 feet 9 inches (wings swept back). Capable of a top speed of about Mach 2.4 when unloaded, the Su-24 has an operational service ceiling of about 57,400 feet and a combat range of just 200 miles when fully loaded with weapons. The aircraft is believed to be equipped with advanced avionics systems, although details are not known. The Su-24 can carry a wide variety of weapons, including a six-barrel 23mm machine gun, various AA- 2 Atoll, AA-8 Aphid and AA-7 Apex air-to-air missiles, tactical air-to-surface missiles, various general purpose bombs weighing up to 2,205 pounds, rocket launchers and anti- runway BETAB-250 bombs.

Tupolev TU-22 Blinder: The Soviet version of this reconnaissance bomber is powered by two afterburning turbojets generating a maximum estimated 30,865 pounds of thrust each. The swept-wing bomber measures 133 feet long, 34 feet tall and weighs in at 185,000 pounds when fully loaded with up to 17,600 pounds of weapons. Top speed is Mach 1.5 with a service ceiling of about 60,000 feet and a combat radius of some 2,000 miles. The bomber version of the Blinder, known as the Tu-22A, is equipped with a bomb bay presumably modified to carry conventional weapons. The Tu-22 saw extensive action during the Iran-Iraq war.

TU-16 Badger: The Tu-16 originally was built to serve as a strategic bomber for the Soviet Union, although it now serves in a variety of roles. The big jet is equipped with a pair of turbojet engines generating 20,950 pounds of thrust each and weighs up to 169,755 pounds fully loaded with weapons and fuel. The bomber measures 109 feet from wingtip to wingtip with a 114-foot-long fuselage. Maximum speed is about 590 mph with a 43,000-foot operational ceiling. The Badger's range, with a full load of weapons, is about 2,980 miles. Up to 19,180 pounds of bombs and other weapons can be accommodated. Three Badgers were destroyed on the ground by coalition forces in the opening week of Operation Desert Storm.

Three F-111 variable-wingsweep strike aircraft in flight. With wings swept back, the F-111 can reach twice the speed of sound; with the wings set at full forward, it can fly low and slow.

A MASSIVE ARMADA

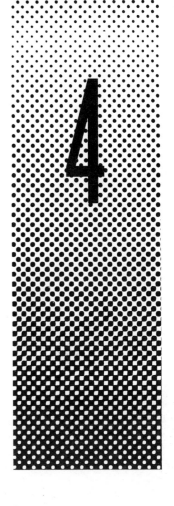

4

The allies assembled an armada of at least 160 naval vessels devoted initially to enforcing the United Nations sanctions on trade with Iraq. They conducted literally thousands of shipping inspections in the weeks leading up to the war and boarded several hundred ships to make sure no war materiel made its way to Saddam. Thirty-six vessels were turned away and in a handful of cases, warning shots were fired. But one of history's most powerful armadas was not in and around the Persian Gulf simply to enforce an economic blockade; it was there to provide the muscle that would be needed in the event negotiations broke down and Saddam refused to quit Kuwait.

The American contribution to the fleet included:

- 108 vessels, including two battleships, six aircraft carriers and at least one nuclear submarine.
- 50,000 American sailors.

Opposite:
A smoke ring hovers above the sea after the test-firing of one of the Wisconsin's twelve five-inch guns. The Wisconsin also has nine 16-inch guns, and carries one of the most advanced and accurate weapons used in the war, the computer-guided Tomahawk cruise missile.

• 500 Tomahawk cruise missiles
• 450 state-of-the-art carrier-based fighters and attack bombers.

Just as the B-52s and carpet-bombing of Republican Guard positions conjured up images of Vietnam, so did the presence of two World War II veterans equipped with the latest in modern weaponry present the sharpest contrast between the old and the new of this century-ending war.

Aboard the USS Wisconsin, the gunner of No. 1 turret yells out instructions during a loading exercise with the 16-inch guns of the recommissioned WW II battleship. The shell and powder fit in the cylinder at right.

ALLIED SHIPS

Battleships: Two 50-year-old battlewagons—BB-63 Missouri and BB-64 Wisconsin—were carrying the Tomahawks that were launched on opening night of the war. Each ship carried 32 of the deadly accurate, robotic flying bombs. In fact, it was a shot of a Tomahawk rising off the deck and streaking into the night sky that found its way into many of the news magazines. Some of the early television footage of the war showed the trail of the rocket launchers of the turbojet weapons illuminating the

battlewagon's still-potent 16-inch guns. While the carriers and their airwings were the glamour boys of the fleet, it was the hulking battleships that represented the raw muscle of the old days.

Both were born in January, 1941, and put in to service in 1944, allowing them to catch the closing days of the war. When the Reagan administration decided it wanted to get the size of the Navy back up to 600 ships from the post-Vietnam low of about 470, it turned to the mothballed battleships, bringing back not only the latest combatants but also the Iowa and the New Jersey. The Iowa suffered a catastrophic turret explosion in 1989 and both it and the New Jersey are being retired. In fact, sometime after the Missouri and the Wisconsin finish their Gulf duty their fate will be the same.

The aging monsters displace about half as much as an aircraft carrier, 46,234 tons empty and 57,500 tons loaded, yet can steam at over 33 knots at flank and just over 30 knots in sustained sailing. The eight boilers driving four geared turbines through four shafts produce 212,000 shaft horsepower.

Three of the USS Wisconsin's 16-inch guns dwarf sailors on the deck of the battleship in the Gulf. The big guns can throw an artillery shell at a target 20 miles away.

The American carrier USS Independence steams into the Gulf of Oman during the build-up to Desert Storm. Lining her decks are fighter planes; in the foreground, F-18 Hornets, with their distinctive angled tailfins.

The Tomahawks and the guns that can hurl 2,700-pound shells about 20 miles constitute the most dramatic part of the ships' armaments, but by no means all of it. The nine booming 16-inchers are accompanied on the 887-foot ships by a full dozen five-inch guns and four Phalanx Close In Weapons Systems, or CIWS (pronounced Sea-Whiz)—Gatling-gun type protective devices that throw a wall of projectiles at anything its radar determines to be a threat. CIWS is intended as a last-ditch close range protection against anti-ship missiles like the French-built Exocet that might slip through the protective net of escort vessels.

Protecting the hull of each battlewagon is foot-thick armor, and the big gun turrets have protection more than 17 inches thick on the facing. On the reshaped fantails is a landing deck for anti-submarine warfare helicopters.

The Missouri was based in Long Beach, Calif., while the Wisconsin was based in Norfolk, Va. A crew of 1,525 was assigned to each ship, making them very labor intensive.

Aircraft Carriers: The carriers, of course, were the behemoths of the conflict, floating fortresses for 5,000 or more, half of them sailors and the other half Navy and Marine aviators and aircraft mechanics. Each carried between 70 to nearly 90 aircraft, depending on the class boat and composition of the air wings.

The nuclear-powered Theodore Roosevelt, the newest of the six carriers in the war, was put into service in October, 1986. Its crew was larger than the others—6,286 officers and enlisted men. Powered by two General Electric pressurized water reactors generating 280,000 shaft horsepower through four props, the Roosevelt's deck measured a full 1,040 feet long and 252 feet wide. Because of its size, it could carry more than 80 aircraft with a typical complement of 20 F-14A Tomcats, 20 F/A-18 Hornets, 20 A-6E Intruders, five EA-6B Prowlers, five E-2C Hawkeyes, 10 S-3A anti- submarine warfare planes and six SH-3H ASW helicopters.

Weighing 96,300 tons when fully loaded, the Roosevelt could make better than 30 knots when steaming into the wind to assist with takeoffs and landings.

Two of the older carriers in the fleet—the Midway and the Ranger— were sent into the narrow Persian Gulf to help provide air cover for the fleet and contribute planes to raids into Kuwait and Iraq from the

Aboard the carrier Kennedy, Lt.Thomas Stubblefield signals the deck edge operator for catapult one to launch an A-7E Corsair II. The crew is training with chemical protective equipment.

Overleaf:
**A pack of of F-19
Tomcats on the carrier's
deck. The Tomcat's
weapons systems can
attack six enemy planes
at once, at distances
close to 100 miles. In
the right foreground is
a blast shield to deflect
exhaust gases during
launch.**

**Air crewmen wash and
scrub a CH-53 Super
Stallion helicopter. The
huge helicopter can fly
at close to 200 mph and
carry up to 56 troops.**

southeast. Both were conventionally powered and their air wings were organized a bit differently.

For instance, the Midway was deployed with no F-14s, but had 36 F/A-18s while the Ranger had 24 F-14s, 24 A-6Es and four of the tanker version of the A-6, the KA-6D.

Joining the Roosevelt in the Red Sea were the America, the John F. Kennedy and the Saratoga, a ship fractionally older than the Ranger.

Cruisers: The cruiser USS Bunker Hill, CG 52, was one of the earlier ships in the Ticonderoga Class and was outfitted with the AEGIS weapons system, a system that suffered a major embarrassment in the Gulf when it tragically was involved in the shoot-down of an Iranian civilian airliner by the USS Vincennes in 1988. Still a very capable system, it gives combat directors an excellent look at what may be coming, from missiles to aircraft, and can operate as a controller for planes in its vicinity. In the case of the Bunker Hill, it also carried the Tomahawk cruise missile. It was the Bunker Hill that was first used to test the vertical launch process for the cruise missile.

Cruisers displace 9,600 tons when fully loaded and their four gas turbines can push them through the warm Gulf waters at better than 30 knots. They are 563 feet long and have a beam of 55 feet. They carry ASW helicopters, the Harpoon and Standard anti-ship missiles, two 5-inch guns, two Phalanx systems and have six torpedo tubes.

Destroyers: The Spruance Class destroyer USS Moosbrugger, based in Charleston, S.C., carried eight Harpoon missiles, the Tomahawk and a battery of torpedoes in addition to the Phalanx, 5-inch guns and the Sea Sparrow. It could make 33 knots and carried two SH-60 anti-submarine warfare helicopters.

Guided Missile Destroyers: Among the combatants, Great Britain sent the guided missile destroyer HMS Gloucester and assigned it to work with the USS Wisconsin operating in the northern Persian Gulf. The Gloucester, powered by Rolls Royce gas turbines, weighed 4,775 tons fully loaded and could hit just over 29 knots in a sprint. It carried a Lynx helicopter, the GWS-30 Sea Dart missile system, two close-in Gatling gun systems and a nearly 5-inch gun that could hurl shells up to 25,000 yards.

Other front-line U.S. warships contributed both to the Tomahawk launch and to the blockade that was thrown up around Iraq immediately after its invasion. The international naval force spent its days and nights intercepting shipping that appeared headed for Iraq and sending boarding parties where necessary.

Minesweepers: One of the most vital classes of ships in the Gulf was the

A CH-46 Sea Knight helicopter flies past the stern of the amphibious transport dock USS Raleigh.

minesweepers, vessels with the dangerous job of seeking out and disabling Iraqi mines, mines so powerful they could send a plume of water hundreds of feet into the air. It was an Iraqi mine that a re-flagged supertanker hit during a Gulf trip under U.S. escort in 1987, and the frigate USS Samuel B. Roberts was nearly broken in half by a mine in April 1988.

Several U.S. Avenger class minesweepers were hauled to the Gulf on a floating dry dock for use in finding and disabling Iraqi mines. The British contributed minesweeping capabilities as well and Germany sent five minesweepers into the region.

The Avenger class, according to the Navy, is a revolutionary concept in mine warfare. The ships have a remotely piloted, tethered mine neutralization system that has sonar, video capability, cable cutters and a detonating device. The ships are sheathed in fiberglass and have a wooden hull to foil mines that are triggered by metal. They are fairly light — displacing 1,312 tons when loaded—and small at just 224 feet in length. They are only 39 feet wide and can only make 13.5 knots. As a further protection, their engines have aluminum blocks. They carry a crew of 74.

The British and West German minesweepers were smaller boats, vessels of about half the displacement of the Avenger and its sister ships.

Five British minesweepers were operating as a unit under the command of the HMS Herald, and typical of them was the HMS

The amphibious assault ship USS Nassau steams alongside the Raleigh. Ships like these would carry troops to the shores of Kuwait in a ground attack on Saddam's troops.

Atherstone. Displacing 770 tons fully loaded, Atherstone was manned by Royal Naval Reserve personnel. It followed the design of North Sea oilfield supply vessels and used the BAJ- Vickers Wire Sweep Mark 9 Team Sweep System. It worked in tandem with another vessel but could also work independently

Submarines: While the Navy would not say how many submarines were involved and where they were located, officials did acknowledge that at least one cruise missile was fired from the Red Sea by the USS Louisville, a Los Angeles-class 688 attack sub based in San Diego, Calif. Such boats measure 360 feet long with a beam of 33 feet and have 12 vertical launch tubes packed into forward buoyancy spaces just behind the sonar dome. Missiles are ejected from the launch tube in a canister that falls free once it pops to the surface. A rocket motor then ignites and once aloft, a small jet engine takes over.

The Louisville, known as SSN-724, was built by General Dynamic's electric boat division in Connecticut, displacing 6,900 tons submerged. The sub was powered by a single nuclear reactor and could do better than 30 knots submerged.

While the subs prowled under the water, Marines bobbed on top of it. The largest Marine amphibious assault force since the famed Inchon landing in Korea was assembled for the Desert Sword slugfest. And they

had their own specialized gear to get them onto the beach and, if necessary, over it.

Assault Craft: The newest tool in the Marine toolbox is the Landing Craft- Air Cushion, or LCAC, a hovercraft capable of being carried by the Landing Ship Dock (LSD) class vessel. The hovercraft each can carry 60 tons, or 75 tons in an overloaded condition. Capable of launching an amphibious assault from over the horizon—LCACs can travel 200 miles at 40 knots—the craft's design lets it slide up over the shore to drop its cargo inland. They displace 200 tons when fully loaded, have a length of 80 feet and a beam of 47, and are powered by four Avco-Lycoming gas turbines. Lift is provided by four double-entry fans and forward propulsion is generated by two reversible pitch propellers on the aft end of the craft.

Many of the Marines were under the command of the USS Blue Ridge out of Yokosuka, Japan, an amphibious command ship with a complement of 720 officers and enlisted personnel. It and its sister ship, the Mount Whitney, were built with the same basic hull as the Iwo Jima-class helicopter carriers, except they have only a helicopter on their fantails and no helicopters in a hanger.

A sailor works on one of the Raleigh's three-inch guns.

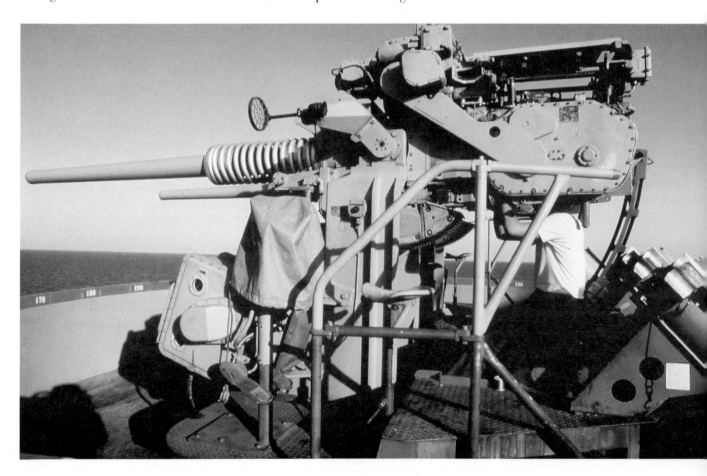

The Blue Ridge, which spent considerable time in the Gulf, was 620 feet long with a beam of 82 feet. It was protected by Sea Sparrow surface-to-air missiles, four three-inch anti-aircraft guns and two of the Phalanx close-in weapons systems. It had been the flagship of the 7th Fleet since 1979.

Typical of the assault ships in the Gulf was the USS Iwo Jima, named after a famed World War II battle, and it was responsible for hauling not only Marines, but also the helicopters they needed for battle.

The Iwo, as it was known, and the USS Okinawa, LPH 3 and LPH 4 respectively, carried eleven CH-53 helicopters. They also carried 20 of the CH-46 Sea Knights for hauling Marines about. The newest versions also are capable of handling the AV-8B Harrier jump jet flown by Marines.

Their self-protection consisted of two cells of eight Sea Sparrows, four 3-inch guns and two of the Phalanx systems. Aboard the two were 685 naval personnel and 2,000 Marines.

The USS Barbour County (LST-1195) based in San Diego, Calif., was making its contribution to the Gulf War as well. A tank landing ship, the Barbour County's job was to haul and land amphibious vehicles, combat vehicles and equipment in amphibious assaults. She was larger and faster than her predecessors, largely because she was equipped with a 112- foot ramp off the top of the bow to disgorge her cargo of heavy equipment and tanks rather than bulky bow doors that kept the earlier ships slow. The Barbour County could make 20 knots. Her stern gate also allowed her to launch amphibious vehicles directly into the water. The Barbour County, with 290 sailors and 400 troops, was defended by four machine guns.

The Barbour County and ships like the USS Whidbey Island, a landing ship dock, carried amphibious assault craft called the AAV7-A1. The Corps had 1,323 such craft in the inventory, each one weighing more than 38,000 pounds. Powered by a turbocharged Cummins Diesel, the AAV7-A1 can carry up to 25 Marines. They also have tracked running gear for the land and two water jets for propulsion at sea. Recent upgrades include night vision devices, smoke generators, applique armor, a stronger transmission and an automatic fire suppression system.

The Whidbey Island was capable of carrying four air-cushion landing craft and its 609-feet length left room for a helicopter pad. It was operated by a Navy crew of 342 and had 500 troops.

Supporting the assault force vessels were the likes of the USS Durham (LKA 114) also out of San Diego. The lightly armed Durham, with a length of 575 feet and a beam of 82 feet, could make 20 knots hauling the heavy equipment and supplies needed for amphibious assaults.

Transport docks like the USS Ogden (LPD-5) from Long Beach, Calif., also were involved in backing up the amphibious troops. They each carried 900 Marines and up to six of the CH-46 Sea Knights. The job of LPD-5 and its sister ships was to transport and land Marines.

CH-53 Super Stallion Helicopter: This is the same huge chopper that was involved eleven years ago, and only a few hundred miles away, in the unsuccessful effort to rescue Americans held hostage in Iran. The CH-53 is capable of carrying between 38 and 56 troops, depending on the model, or 24 litter patients with four medics. It has a three-man crew and the seven-bladed rotor folds for deck storage. The craft is slightly more than 99 feet long, has a maximum speed of 196 mph and can hit 27,900

The USS Tattnall steams north through the Suez Canal.

feet in horizontal flight or hover at 16,600. The range is 552 miles but the Sikorsky-built chopper can be ferried 1,138 miles.

Command and Control: The command ship of the Middle East Task Force, the USS La Salle, began its life as a landing platform dock ship and was modified for use as the flagship. Placed in service in 1964, the La Salle displaced 14,650 tons when fully loaded. Equipped with light armor and two Babcock & Wilcox boilers, the La Salle was manned by 25 officers and 445 men plus a flag staff of 12 officers and 47 enlisted personnel. It had a helicopter hangar on the after deck. She was affectionately known as the "Great White Ghost" because of her all-white paint scheme. To support her command responsibilities the La Salle was equipped with two satellite communication antennas.

Hospital Ships: Hoping for the best but prepared for the worst, the Navy dispatched two 1,000-bed hospital ships, the Mercy and Comfort, to the Persian Gulf, possibly off the coast near Bahrain. Both were converted San Clemente-class merchant tankers that were placed into service in 1987. The Mercy, based in Oakland, Calif., once was known as the tanker Worth. The Comfort, based in Baltimore, Md., once went by the name Rose City. Both ships are painted bright white with large red crosses on either side and on the upper decks. The center of each hospital ship was equipped with a large helicopter landing platform and area for boat stowage. Each had 12 operating rooms, four X-ray rooms, 80 beds for intensive care and 1,000 ward beds.

It was to the Mercy and the Comfort that some soldiers and Marines wounded in the ground campaign would come after initial treatment at the battlefield MASH units or more rearward facilities.

THE IRAQI NAVY

Iraq's naval force, badly damaged in early skirmishes with allied forces, was negligible to start with. Saddam Hussein began the war with four Italian-built frigates, each displacing no more than 2,525 tons when provisioned for battle. There was a training frigate, lightly armored, and four guided missile frigates. They had five-inch guns and the Albatros SAM system along with the Otomat Mark II surface-to-surface missile. And they carried two AB-212 anti-submarine warfare helicopters.

Iraq also had four guided missile corvettes, 10 guided missile patrol boats and a variety of small patrol boats, most bought from the Soviet Union and other Eastern Bloc nations. The Iraqi vessels were largely ineffective against the allied armada and several small patrol boats were sunk in the early days of the war.

Overleaf:
The carrier USS Saratoga sails by a mosque at the Red Sea town of Suez. In the center of the photograph are the radar domes of two E-2C Hawkeye planes, which act as airborne control centers for air defense and attack.

THE GROUND WARRIORS

5

A llied leaders suspected from the begining that air power alone would not be enough to budge Saddam from Kuwait. A ground campaign was likely - so the planners prepared for one of the most intensive tank battles they could imagine.

America's M-1A1s, Britain's Challengers and Chieftains and France's AMX-30s were shipped in to combine the best of old fashioned hardware with modern targeting computer software, the kind of electronic wizardry that lets the U.S. Abrams fire at speeds of up to 20 mph.

Softening up areas of potential battle was the mission of the thousands of artillery tubes brought in for the assault. The job of Navy and Marine airpower was to rake the beaches where air cushion landing craft were brought in to help thousands of Marines skim ashore in a novel new form of the battle-tested amphibious landing. And multiple launch rocket tubes were designed to lay waste to huge patches of Iraqi defenses with the kind of power that leaves not a single thing standing, not a single thing living.

Opposite:
A tank from Britain's 7th Armored Brigade moves through the desert while a Lynx helicopter hovers overhead. The brigade, known as the 'Desert Rats,' was practicing live fire maneuvers.

An M-1A1 Abrams tank on patrol. The state of the art in armored fighting vehicles, the M-1A1 can hit a target over a mile distant while moving at 20 mph. The tank beams a laser at its target; its computer calculates the range while other sensors gauge crosswinds, air density, and any degree of droop in the gun barrel if it has heated from firing. The M-1A1 is protected against artillery, chemical and biological weapons, and nuclear fallout.

Then, and only then, planners said, would the infantryman be sent onto the field of battle, protected initially by a wide array of armored personnel carriers and infantry fighting vehicles that have been developed for the modern battlefield. Saddam apparently planned to force the allies into ground fighting ahead of their schedule, sending Iraqi troops probing into Saudi territory at Khafji. They succeeded in drawing blood from the allied defenders but were finally repulsed with heavy losses in men and machines.

The final pieces of the air-land battle doctrine: the so-ugly-it's-beautiful A-10 Warthog jet and the Cobra and Apache helicopters, all tank killers able to fire from over the horizon, invisible to the front line. Not to be overlooked was the E-8 J-Stars surveillance plane capable of painting a radar map of the battlefield and giving ground commanders a picture not only of what's in front but also what's coming up from the rear.

All this hardware except the fixed-wing aircraft were hurriedly shipped into a port in Eastern Saudi Arabia that cannot be identified, a port where helicopters arrived shrink-wrapped, where pallets of high explosives were lifted from break-bulk ships and tanks were brought out of the RORO or roll-on, roll-off ships.

North of the Saudi town of Hafr-al-Batin, just south of the Kuwait-Iraq-Saudi border, lies a broad plain through which nomadic bedouins and spice traders have roamed. It is an area of hard packed dirt so flat and so devoid of any natural features that standing and looking at the empty horizon can produce a feeling of abandonment and a sense of being able to see the curve of the Earth. It is also an area where some massive firepower was displayed, ready for a potential race up the Wadi al-Batin, the valley left from an ancient river that roughly delineates the Iraqi-Kuwaiti border. It is a natural attack route around the back of Kuwait up toward Republican Guard positions and an absolutely natural jumping off place for the tank battle of the century.

The cornerstones of the allied tank corps were the U.S. M-1A1 Abrams and England's Challenger. The capabilities of each are amazing.

"We own the night," the Army is fond of saying, and the Abrams was a prime tool in the night-fighting arsenal.

"God created the M-1 for this desert."
—Army Lt. Col. Mike Burton, commander,
4-34 Battalion of 3rd Armored Division.

M-1A1 Abrams Main Battle Tank: A rolling fortress that radiates menacing power, the four- man M-1A1 weighs in at 63 tons and measures 26 feet long, 11.8 feet wide and 7.8 feet high to the tip of its squat turret. The tank's primary weapon is a 120mm M-68E1 smoothbore cannon that fires M-728 armor-piercing shells up to 2.5 miles while rumbling along at 20 mph. Other armament includes two 7.62mm M-240 machine guns and one .50-caliber Browning M-2HB machine gun. With its powerful

Soldiers of the 82nd Airborne division ride on an M-551 Sheridan tank.

1,500- horsepower gas turbine engine, the M-1A1 has a top speed of about 42 mph, consuming fuel at the prodigious rate of six gallons per mile. Even so, the M-1A1 has a range of about 288 miles.

The M-1A1's crew compartment is equipped with chemical, biological and nuclear fallout protection, a major advantage over earlier M-1 tanks. The Abrams also can carry more ammunition than its predecessor, 40 rounds, and it is equipped with an advanced carbon-dioxide laser rangefinder, a thermal viewing for night fighting and a better suspension than earlier versions. The M-1A1 fires two types of armor- piercing ammunition and all in all, the M-1A1 is considered the most sophisticated and capable main battle tank in the world.

The United States initially deployed 1,200 M-1A1s on the front lines for Operation Desert Storm with another 700 chemically-vulnerable M-1s held in the rear. The initial M-1s had a 105mm cannon, but it was upgraded with the A1 model to standardize it with European tanks and to let it pack a bigger punch. Despite being outnumbered by an Iraqi force of 4,200 tanks in the Desert Sword theater, the M-1A1 and its coalition counterparts—the British Challenger and French AMX-30—were considered more than a match for Saddam Hussein.

The driver of an M-551 Sheridan tank takes a drink. The Sheridan's gun can fire either a 152mm round or a Shillelagh missile.

M-60 Main Battle Tank: More than 15,000 M-60s were built before production ended in 1987 with most now in use with the Marine Corps. Like the M- 1A1, M-60s now feature chemical, biological and nuclear protection for the four-man crew and night vision gear to allow combat in low-light conditions. The M-60 features the L-7A1 105mm M-68 main gun, a 7.62mm NATO M-73 machine gun and a .50-caliber M-85

machine gun. A 750-horsepower engine produces a top speed of 30 mph and a combat range of 298 miles. The M-60 weighs 57.3 tons and measures 22.6 feet long, 11.8 feet wide and 10.7 feet tall. Its main gun fires the same ammunition as the M-1. Marine Corps M-60s, once in Saudi Arabia, were given reactive armor plating to increase the protection for the tanks.

British Challenger Main Battle Tank: The Challenger is Britain's best tank, a powerhouse in the same class with the M-1A1 and a definite asset in Operation Desert Storm. Great Britain deployed 170 Challengers in Saudi Arabia with the famed "Desert Rats" of the 7th Armored Brigade. (Each tank bears a picture of a red rat.) Equipped with a Rolls Royce Condor V-12 diesel engine, the Challenger's punch comes from a 120mm L-115A rifled cannon and two 7.62mm machine guns. The Challenger measures 27.4 feet long, 11.25 feet wide and 8.16 feet tall and carries a crew of four. Top speed is about 35 mph and the tank has a range of about 250 miles.

Chieftain Main Battle Tank: The Chieftain is equipped with a 120mm L-115A rifled main gun, two 7.62mm machine guns and a single 12.7mm ranging machine gun. With a crew of four, the 60.6-ton Chieftain's top speed is 30 mph with a Leyland Mark-8A engine giving a range of about 300 miles. The Chieftain measures 24.7 feet long, 10.1 feet wide and 9.5 feet tall. It has been in service since 1963.

Next to the A-10 Warthog, the Apache helicopter is the U.S.'s most deadly tank-killer. Visible in the Apache's nose are its night-vision sensors. They feed data in to the crew's helmets, where it appears on a screen inside their visors.

Below:
U.S. Marines in combat at Khafji. Iraqi troops held the Saudi border town for 36 hours in the first real ground engagement of the war. Here Marines from the 1st Division fire 155mm howitzers at Iraqi positions.

AMX-30 Main Battle Tank: The French AMX-30 features a rifled 105mm main gun, a 20mm air defense cannon and a 7.62mm machine gun, weighing in at 39.7 tons (40.8 tons for the AMX-30 B-2). A Renault Hispano- Suiza 110 water-cooled 12-cylinder engine produces a top speed of 40 mph and a combat range of up to 372 miles. The four-man tank measures 21.6 feet long, 10.1 feet wide and 7.5-feet tall to the tip of its turret.

King of the U.S. helicopter assets in a land war is the AH- 64 Apache, successor to the AH-1 Cobra of Vietnam. And the other battlefield powerhouse is the A-10 Warthog.

AH-64 Apache: Hanging on a four-bladed main rotor, the Apache is a tank- killer armed with up to 16 Hellfire missiles, a 30mm Hughes M-230A1 chain gun and a 1,200-round magazine and its four hard points can also carry pods of Hydra 70 rockets.

It has a maximum speed of 186 mph and a maximum cruise of 182 mph, it has a range of 428 miles and an endurance of just under 2 hours. It has twin turbines and a crew of two. It weighs 17,650 pounds fully loaded and is armored in key areas to stop rounds of up to 23mm.

There is a night vision device for the pilot and a target acquisition designation sight for the weaponry. It can follow ground terrain and is equipped with infrared suppression devices, a laser detector, a variety of jamming and chaff and flare dispensers and it also has forward-looking-infrared gear for night-fighting. It often works in tandem with the OH-58

An OH-58D Kiowa Scout helicopter takes off. The sphere atop its rotor shaft houses a laser sighting device that can guide missiles from other aircraft, such as one of the Apaches in the background.

A Multiple Launch Rocket System (MLRS) in Saudi Arabia. The MLRS can fire its 12 rockets in less than 60 seconds, raining down destruction on an area of 50 acres, perhaps over 20 miles away.

Kiowa Scout which can provide target data from its mast-mounted sight.

Hellfire Missile: A third-generation anti-armor weapon, the Hellfire homes in on a laser spot that can be aimed either from the attacking Apache or from a ground observer, allowing the Apache to launch its missiles indirectly without ever seeing the target. It weighs just under 100 pounds and is 7 inches in diameter.

AH-1 Cobra: Cobras scored some of the first kills of Iraqi armored vehicles during the Khafji battle. The Cobra, predecessor to the Apache, is a twin-rotor close support and attack helicopter that can dash across the battlefield at up to 207 mph, depending upon the model. It can travel 357 miles with a full load of fuel and a crew of two and it weighs up to 14,000 pounds when fully loaded. It is built on the basic airframe as the venerable UH-1 Huey.

It is typically armed with a 7.62mm minigun and a 40mm grenade launcher, or a 20mm six-barrel or 30mm three-barrel cannon. And, on its pylons it can hang 76 2.75-inch rockets, minigun pods or a 20mm gun pod, or even eight TOW (tube launched, optically tracked, wire-guided) missiles.

The main rotor has a diameter of 58 feet on the most recent model. The single engine on some of the latest versions produces 2,050 horsepower.

OH-58D Kiowa Scout: The all-weather Kiowa is the first true scout helicopter of the Army's helicopter fleet. Atop its main rotor is a sighting device that looks like a deep sea diver's helmet. It contains a laser designator that can be used for Hellfire missiles and other laser homing weapons to track in on. The sighting device can enable the helicopter to stay below the protection of a ridge line or dune, with the optics peering over the top and sighting enemy targets.

Built around the basic airframe of a Bell helicopter, it has 650 horsepower engine. It is very lightly armed, but later models will come equipped with the air-to-air version of the Stinger missile and some air-to-ground missiles.

A-10 Thunderbolt: Affectionately known as the "Warthog," this boxy-looking ground support attack plane's claim to fame is an evil-looking GAU-8/A Avenger 30mm seven-barrel Gatling gun built to destroy tanks and other enemy assets on the ground. In fact, some observers have described the A-10 as an airframe built around the Avenger. The Warthog also can carry up to 16,000 pounds of mixed ordnance, including 500-pound parachute-retarded bombs, 2,000-pound general purpose explosives, Maverick missiles, incendiary bombs, Rockeye-23 cluster bombs and laser-guided or TV-operated smart bombs.

For self defense, the A-10 is equipped with infrared countermeasure flares to decoy enemy SAMs, chaff to mislead radar homing missiles and electronic jamming equipment. With a bullet-proof canopy, the cockpit is surrounded by titanium armor, protecting the pilot from hits of armor-piercing 23mm shells. Other critical flight control systems also are protected.

The A-10 is equipped with two 8,900-pound-thrust turbofan engines and is capable of a top speed of about 420 mph at 5,000 feet when carrying six Mark 82 general purpose bombs. With a wingspan of 57 feet 6 inches, the A-10 is 53 feet 4 inches long and stands 14 feet 8 inches tall. The aircraft, weighing 50,000 pounds fully loaded, has a range of about 250 miles when carrying 9,500 pounds of weaponry. The plane is extremely agile down low and can turn exceptionally tight circles, almost standing on its wingtip just above a battlefield to maneuver and hit tanks.

GAU-8/A Avenger Cannon: The most powerful machine gun ever mounted on an airplane, the 21-foot-long Avenger fires 30mm slugs nearly the size of a soft-drink bottle at a velocity of 3,500 feet per second. The recoil from the gun is so great that it quickly slows the A-10 down. For that reason, and to prevent the recoil from causing the nose of the A-10 to pitch up, the gun is aimed slightly downward and offset to the left so the active barrel is lined up on the plane's center line. The Avenger can fire up to 3,900 rounds of armor-piercing bullets per minute and can be loaded with explosive ammo for use against trucks and other targets.

A soldier in chemical protective gear.

Hawk missiles at an unidentified desert site. The radar-guided Hawk is considered one of the allies' most dependable weapons against attacking aircraft.

OV-10 Bronco: A Marine Corps observation and reconnaissance aircraft, the Bronco also helps support air and ground units of landing forces. Built by Rockwell, the plane has a pilot and supporting arms coordinator and it is powered with two Garret Research T-76-G-10 turbines hitched to props. It weighs 9,908 pounds loaded for combat. With a wingspan of 40 feet and length of 41 feet 7 inc hes, it can hit 281 mph when flying without external ordnance and it can cover a 228 nautical mile combat radius.

The Bronco carries four 7.62mm machine guns. And it can haul bombs, rockets, gun pods, Sidewinders and extra fuel tanks on five wing and fuselage armament points.

Capable of short takeoffs and landings from unimproved strips or even floating platforms, the Bronco can operate in low ceilings and low visibility conditions and has the FLIR sensor to help work in poor weather. And a cargo bay in back can be used for paradrops or emergency aerial re-supply missions.

J-Stars: At the request of Desert Storm commander Gen. Norman Schwarzkopf, the Air Force rushed its two developmental E-8A aircraft to Saudi Arabia after successful tests in Europe.

Known as the Joint Surveillance Target Attack Radar System or J-Stars, it can give an Army battlefield commander an edge by letting him know about troop, tank and helicopter movements up to 120 miles from the surveillance plane. The system is built into a Boeing 707.

The plane's radar and 17 operating consoles are connected by an electronic data link with a ground station that the Army uses, and movements spotted by the operators are relayed to commanders on the ground.

It carries a crew of 34 and has 17 operating stations. Built by the Grumman Corp., the plane also can be used to track surface ships and slow flying aircraft.

SPECIAL OPERATIONS, INTELLIGENCE ASSETS

Quick Fix: Based on the UH-60 Blackhawk, three different varieties of Quick Fix choppers can fly over a battlefield or behind enemy lines and listen for and jam an enemy's radios.

First Sgt. Randy Hackaday of the U.S. Army's Air Defense Artillery demonstrates the Stinger anti-aircraft missile, just one day before Operation Desert Storm began. The shoulder-fired missile homes in on engine heat.

Overleaf:
Baghdad during the first night of Desert Storm. The Iraqis' anti-aircraft fire lit up the sky, 'like a hundred Fourth of Julys' in the words of one American pilot, but was mostly ineffective.

Opposite:
U.S. Marine Lance Corporal John Clark prepares to fire a mortar shell during live fire practice a few days before the war began. The white spots on the allies' camouflage uniforms mimic the small pebbles that are strewn all over the desert.

A group of SA-2 anti-aircraft missile launchers in the desert.

MH-60K and MH-47E: Both equipped for aerial refueling, they can make low-level night and adverse weather flights for special operations troops and can even carry out clandestine rescue operations. They carry the FLIR sensor suite and the cockpits are designed to minimize pilot workload. Without refueling, the MH-47E can stay up 9.8 hours and the MH-60K can stay aloft 7.6 hours. The MH-47E can haul 42 troops and the smaller MH-60K can take along 12 commandos. Both are armed with two .50-caliber machine guns.

ARTILLERY/AIR DEFENSE

It is essential to be able to keep the airspace overhead clear, and to have the ability to pound the front lines of an opponent with rockets to soften them up for an attack.

The United States, the allies and the Iraqis have a variety of

relatively standard artillery pieces, like 105mm howitzers towed behind various vehicles and the self-propelled 155mm monsters.

Typical of them is the Army's M-119 105mm howitzer. It can fire high explosive, smoke and illumination rounds. It can hurl a standard shell 8.7 miles and a rocket-assisted shell 12.1 miles. It takes a crew of seven to operate the 4,000 pound weapon, which can be towed or sling-loaded beneath a helicopter. The self-propelled 155mm howitzer can hurl a standard shell over 11 miles.

Multiple Launch Rocket System or MLRS: This especially deadly U.S. weapon system can fire a dozen rockets in less than 60 seconds, spreading up to 8,000 bomblets over an area the size of four football fields. The 13-foot-long, 9-inch-wide rockets are mounted in two six- missile canisters carried by a self-propelled launcher- loader. The three-man crew of the MLRS can reload the launcher without leaving the protection of the vehicle, which can move about at 40 mph when necessary. MLRS missiles weigh about 600 pounds and have a range of more than 18 miles.

Hawk: The Hawk is a medium-range air defense system to hit low and medium altitude aircraft attacking an allied position. It can be moved about, operated in all weather and is extremely reliable. It can get to altitudes of more than 33,000 feet and travel more than 19 miles.

The Hawk, deployed worldwide, comes with an acquisition radar, a tracking system, a device to help determine if the approaching plane is a friend or foe (IFF for Identification Friend or Foe), and each launcher has three missiles. A typical battery has three or four launchers. The missiles are guided by reflected radar energy and use a proximity fuse to trigger the warhead. Iraq captured some U.S. Hawks sold to Kuwait, but they are believed to have deteriorated from lack of proper maintenance .

Chaparral: The Chaparral is a short-range air defense and surface-to-surface missile. It is self-propelled, and the missile is a lightweight, supersonic missile that can be aimed, fired and forgotten. It uses passive infrared homing and has the IFF system to keep it from hitting friendly aircraft. A new smokeless rocket motor has been developed for the missile.

Stinger: The Stinger is a shoulder-fired infrared homing missile for air defense at short ranges. It seeks out the heat trail of jet and propeller engines, using a computer to calculate an intercepting course. It also has the IFF feature to ensure it does not knock down friendly aircraft. A tone tells the operator a target has been locked onto, and when the trigger is pulled, a small motor punches the missile out of its launch tube. Once safely away from the gunner a larger rocket fires off. It was first deployed in Germany in 1981.

ARMORED PERSONNEL CARRIERS

In conjunction with the tanks, it is the thousands of infantrymen and Marines who must take and hold the ground after battle commences. Both sides have a variety of protective systems to get the fighting men to the front. The task of the armored personnel carriers and infantry fighting vehicles is to travel close behind the tanks, letting the troops jump out for the close-quarter fighting if necessary.

Bradley Fighting Vehicle: The Bradley is a tracked vehicle with light armor that can be used by scout and armored cavalry units to screen troops and for reconnaissance. There are two varieties, the M-2 infantry fighting vehicle and the M-3 cavalry fighting vehicle.

Both have a two-man turret carrying a 25mm cannon, and they carry the TOW anti-tank weapon along with a 7.62 coaxial machinegun. the M-2 model and its various upgrades also have six 5.56mm firing port weapons along the side and rear of the vehicle.

Its mobility is comparable to the M-1 tank. It can travel at 38 mph and ford bodies of water at 4.4 mph. It has a range of 300 miles and the 60,000 pound vehicle is powered by a 600 horsepower diesel engine. It is 21.5 feet long, 10.5 feet wide and 9.75 feet high. In addition, many have reactive armor on the exterior to help improve survivability. It can climb a 60 percent slope. The M-2 carries a three-man crew and six infantrymen. The M-3 has a three-man crew and two scouts.

The newest models, in addition to the applique armor, have spall liners to reduce the danger of shrapnel from penetrating rounds and rearranged storage for the fuel and ammunition, changes dictated after widely publicized flaps over Pentagon testing .

M-113A3: The M-113A3 is the upgraded armored personnel carrier of the U.S. military, and it can be outfitted with a variety of weapons such as the TOW missile. One version even has a Chaparral SAM launcher added. It can be used to haul troops, equipment and cargo during combat missions and the newest model the A-3, has the spall liner in it.

The fully-tracked vehicle is armored with aluminium, and has external fuel tanks and an upgraded engine and transmission to take the added weight of the spall liner and outside tanks. It weighs 27,200 pounds, is armed with a 50 caliber machine gun and 2,000 rounds of ammunition, and has 275 horsepower. It has a top speed on the road of 42 mph, travels cross country at 20 mph and can carry 13 troops. It can

An U.S. Air Force C5A transport plane ready to unload supplies at a Saudi Arabian airstrip.

Above:
**Paratroopers from the
82nd Airborne division
man a .50-caliber
machine gun.**

ford water areas at 3-6 mph and has a range of 300 miles. It can climb a 2 foot obstacle, get over a 5.5 foot trench and climb a 60 percent slope.

Light Armored Vehicle LAV-25: Used both by the Army and the Marine Corps, the LAV as it is known carries a 25mm cannon and a 7.62mm machine gun in its rearward turret. It travels on eight huge tires and can hit 62 mph on land and 6.5 mph in the water. It has a cruising range of 400 miles and can go straight up a 60 percent slope or across a 30 percent hill.

It carries 71 gallons of fuel, weighs 28,400 pounds, has a crew of seven including four infantrymen and its turret can be depressed 8 degrees.

The LAV-25 is the centerpiece of the light armored infantry battalion. It is widely used for reconnaissance, and its cannon fires armor piercing rounds, incendiary traces and it can take on Soviet-built BMP personnel carriers at 2,750 yards. It is 21 feet long, 7.2 feet wide and 8.2 feet high.

LVTP-7: Also used by the Marine Corps, the tracked vehicle can carry up to 25 personnel and has a crew of three. It has a 12.7mm machine gun, weighs 52,768 pounds, has a range of 300 miles and can go at 45 mph on

Marine Corps M-60 tanks. The rectangular plates on their turrets is reactive armor, which actually explodes when hit by a high energy antitank (HEAT) weapon. The explosion disrupts the effect of an incoming HEAT round.

A TOW missile launcher atop a humvee under camouflage netting. When fired, the missile is steered by signals passed along a wire that unreels behind it.

the road and 8.4 mph in the water. While it runs on tracks on the land, it uses water jets, one on each side of the hull, to get through the water.

The newest versions are equipped with smoke generators, night vision equipment, and better crew and troop compartment ventilation. The seats stow so the vehicle can be used as an ambulance or to haul cargo.

British MCV-80: Armed with a 30mm Rarden cannon and a 7.62mm coaxial chain gun, the 20.8-foot-long APC weighs 52,910 pounds and is powered by a Rolls Royce V-8 diesel that puts out 550 horsepower. The fully-tracked vehicle can travel at just over 46 mph, can travel 310 miles, span an 8-foot trench and climb a 60 percent grade. The vehicle has a crew of two and can carry eight soldiers.

AMX-10: France also has an APC, the AMX-10 which carries a crew of three and eight soldiers. Armed with a 20mm cannon and a coaxial 7.62mm machine gun, it can hit 40 mph on the open road and over 4 mph in the water. It is lighter than other countries' versions at 31,300 pounds, most likely because it is made of welded aluminium. Each soldier has a periscope with which to look out of the fully tracked vehicle.

ANTI-TANK MISSILES

Destroying tanks is a critical element of any modern land battle and the United Nations coalition fields a variety of especially nasty weapons to knock out enemy firepower.

Dragon: The Dragon medium-range wire-guided anti-tank missile is a highly-accurate shoulder-launched rocket that is particularly useful at the platoon level. The operator merely sights on the target through a cross-hair scope and then fires. Sensors in the 6.5-pound launcher then track the heat given off by the rocket motor and send course-correction commands to the missile through thin wires that trail out behind it. The missile weighs 24.5 pounds and has a range of 3,000 feet.

TOW 2: At Khafji, TOWs were successful in hammering Iraqi armor. A portable heavy anti-tank weapon, the tube-launched, optically-tracked, wire-guided—TOW—missile is extremely effective in delivering shaped-charge explosives to their targets. Once a soldier selects a target, the missile is fired, trailing wires behind it that are used to route commands from the launcher to the rocket's steering fins. Each TOW missile is about 4.6 feet long, 6 inches wide and weighs some 47.4 pounds at launch. It can hit targets up to 12,000 feet away at speeds up to 625 mph.

IRAQI WEAPONS

Saddam Hussein spent some $50 billion of his nation's scarce revenues over the past decade assembling what many say is the fourth-largest military machine on Earth, all for a country with roughly 16 million people. Although his inventory contains some older U.S. and allied equipment, it was to Moscow that he turned for the bulk of his most modern weaponry. His holdings include:

T-72 Main Battle Tank: The Soviet-built T-72 is a formidable battlefield

A group of U.S. Marines with their humvee. Burning in the distance is an oil depot on the Kuwaiti border that was hit by Iraqi artillery on January 17. Marine helicopters later attacked the Iraqi positions and destroyed the artillery.

asset with a giant 125mm smoothbore 2A-465 main gun, a 7.62mm machine gun and a 12.7mm machine gun. The T-72 tips the scales at 45.2 tons and measures 22.6 feet long, 11.8 feet wide and 7.7 feet tall. Carrying a crew of three, this three-man Soviet stalwart is powered by a 12-cylinder diesel engine developing 780 horsepower for a top speed of about 37 mph. The T-72's operational combat range is about 298 miles. It has been in operation since 1977 and Iraq reportedly had between 500 and 1,000 of them entering the war. It also had 30 British-built Chieftains.

T-62 Main Battle Tank: Another Soviet import, the four-man T-62 battle tank has been around since 1961. It is equipped with a 115mm U-5TS smoothbore cannon and two machine guns identical to the ones carried by the T-72. Weighing 44 tons, the T-62 measures 21.7 feet long, 10.8 feet wide and 7.8 feet tall. It is equipped with a 580-horsepower V-

12 diesel giving it a top speed of about 31 mph and a combat range of some 280 miles. The Iraqis had about 1,500 of the T-62s. The rest of its tank force was composed of lesser quality, older vintage tanks.

Mi-24 Hind: The backbone of Iraq's attack helicopter corps was about 40 of the famed Soviet Mi-24 Hind attack helicopters that saw extensive service in Afghanistan. Powered by two 2,220 shaft horsepower turboprops, the five-bladed main rotor is almost 56 feet in diameter. The plane under a normal load weighs 22,046 pounds, and it has a maximum speed of 199 mph. With a maximum weapons load it has a combat range of just 99 miles.

The typical Hind is equipped with a 12.7mm gun in the nose, and its two stubby wings can hold four wire-guided anti-tank missiles and four other pods holding bombs, missiles, rockets or guns. And it can also serve as a troop carrier, with room inside for up to eight troops and their gear. It is not as maneuverable as the allied attack helicopters.

Iraq also had in its inventory the lesser-known Bo-105, the SA-316, the SA-321, some with Exocet missiles, and the SA-342.

Anti-Aircraft Guns: Iraq had at least 4,000 air defense guns, including the 23mm ZSU-23-4, a self-propelled, radar-directed gun that can throw a shell more than 8,000 feet. Also in its inventory was the ZSU-57-2, a 55mm weapon that also is self-propelled and can get a shell up 12,000 feet. It is built on the chassis of a T-54 tank. Iraq also had a variety of towed anti-aircraft guns.

MISSILES

A major element in any land war is preventing enemy warplanes from achieving air superiority over the battlefield. The Iraqi army and air force fielded a variety of Soviet-made surface-to-air missiles—SAMs—to knock down coalition aircraft. While exact numbers were impossible to obtain, the Iraqi military, in theater and out, was believed to have a total SAM force of about 160 SA-2s, 140 SA-3s, some 300 SA-6, -7, -8, -9, -14s and 100 Roland self-propelled air defense missile systems. In addition , the Iraqis were thought to have, in total, 4,000 air defense guns of various sizes. Massive anti-aircraft batteries were in place around Baghdad. The following examples illustrate the capabilities of the SAM systems in place in Iraq:

SA-7: The SA-7 is a heat-seeking shoulder-launched missile capable of hitting aircraft up to 6.25 miles away. Operation is simple and straight-forward. The soldier first aims the launch tube at a target and lightly pulls the trigger to activate the missile's infrared seeker. Once the sensor "locks on," a red light changes to green and the soldier pulls the trigger. A solid-fuel charge fires the rocket out of the launch tube and after it is a safe distance away, a solid-fuel motor ignites, pushing the warhead to Mach 1.5. The SA-7 is in wide use around the world.

SA-8: The Soviet-built SA-8 is made up of four radar- or infrared-guided missiles mounted on an amphibious vehicle along with search and guidance radars. The missiles are 10.5 feet long, 8.25 inches in diameter and weigh about 420 pounds before launch, hitting a top speed of Mach 2 with a range of about 40,000 feet. Along with the four missiles loaded on a launcher, eight spares are believed to be carried inside the SA-8 vehicle.

Roland: The Roland self-propelled missile defense system is in wide use around the world, including Iraq. In the French army, the Roland missile launcher is mounted on the chassis of an AMX- 30 main battle tank. The West German army uses the Marder armored personnel carrier chassis while the U.S. Army employs the chassis of an M-109 155mm self-

Pvt. Nathanial Callis of the U.S. Army's VII Corps leans against the gun of his Abrams tank. On the gun barrel the crew has written a message for Saddam Hussein: "C-Ya in Baghdad.'

propelled howitzer as the Roland platform. Roland missiles measure 7.8 feet long, 6.3 inches in diameter and weigh 147 pounds at launch. They can be optically or radar guided with a range of about 4 miles and a service ceiling of 16,400 feet.

SURFACE-TO-SURFACE MISSILES

FROG-7: The Soviet-built FROG-7, an acronym for "free rocket over ground," is a tactical missile mounted on a ZIL-135 transporter with a single quickly raised launch rail and an on-board crane for speedy reloading. The FROG-7 measures 30 feet long and about 2 feet in diameter with a launch weight of some 5,500 pounds. It has a range of up to 9.3 miles.

SCUD: A Soviet-built liquid-fueled rocket, the Scud is a ballistic surface-to-surface missile. A description can be found in chapter 3.

Multiple launch rocket systems of various types are in use in virtually all major military forces around the world and Iraq is no exception. The Iraqi army was equipped with 200 such launchers using rockets of various sizes, but details about their deployment in the Kuwaiti theater was not known. Here are details about a typical Iraqi system:

122mm BM-21—The widely-used Soviet-made BM-21 consists of a Ural-375 truck, a 40-round launcher and 40 9-foot-long, 100-pound missiles, all of which can be fired in less than 30 seconds to hit a target with up to 1 ton of high explosives. The rockets also can carry chemical weapons and the launcher can reach an elevation of 50 degrees and rotate 120 degrees about its base. Reloading takes less than 15 minutes.

ARTILLERY

Among the Soviet systems in the Iraqi inventory is the D-30 122mm howitzer. It has a range of 9.5 miles and because the shell is larger, it is significantly more lethal than the 105mm system. The Iraqi system also requires a crew of seven. Iraq also has earlier models of the U.S.-built 155mm howitzer.

Armored Personnel Systems: Iraq owns 6,000 APCs and Pentagon sources said when the war started about 2,800 of them were in the Kuwaiti theater. Among Saddam's stocks are some U.S.-built M-113 A-1 and A-2 models, meaning they lack the spall liners and external fuel tanks.

The Soviet-built MT-LB has a crew of two and can carry 11 soldiers. Armed with a 7.62mm machine gun, the 21-foot-long vehicle weighs 26,234 pounds when loaded for combat. The 240 horsepower V-8 diesel can get the tracked vehicle up to 38 mph on the road. It can travel just over 3 mph in the water and can climb a 60 percent slope. It is far lower that other APCs, has a range of 310 miles and can be used to tow artillery.

Anti-Tank Weapons: The Iraqi army also is equipped with a variety of anti-tank weapons, chiefly the Soviet-built AT-3 Sagger and AT-4 Spigot. In basic design they are similar to Western anti-tank weapons, portable and wire-guided. The AT-3, with a range of up to 3,280 yards, weighs about 25 pounds. At close ranges it is guided by eye but at longer ranges the target is viewed through a periscopic sight that magnifies the field of view. The wire-guided AT-4 has a range of up to 2,700 yards. It fires a 120mm round that can penetrate armor of up to 600mm.

At a news conference one week into the conflict, Gen. Powell outlined the coalition strategy for ending Saddam's stranglehold on Kuwait:

"This is an air-land-sea campaign, not just an air campaign which at some point will end and then something else starts. It is a single, coherent, integrated air-land-sea campaign. Our strategy to go after this army (in Kuwait) is very, very simple. First, we're going to cut it off. And then we're going to kill it."

"I just want everybody to know that we have a toolbox that's full of lots of tools and I brought them all to the party."
- Gen. Colin Powell,
Chairman, Joint Chiefs of Staff

Overleaf:
The U.N. coalition had struck Iraq with the greatest concentration of the most advanced armaments ever seen on earth. But as a real ground war loomed and the casualties mounted, it was clear that besides the high-tech equipment, the fighting spirit and skill of the troops on both sides would still be the most important weapons of war.